SO-AYT-863

A DUNKER GUIDE TO

BRETHREN HISTORY

Brethren Press

A Dunker Guide to Brethren History
© 2010 Brethren Press

Published by Brethren Press®. Brethren Press is a trademark of the Church of the Brethren, 1451 Dundee Avenue, Elgin, Illinois 60120. Visit www.brethrenpress.com for publishing information.

All rights reserved. No portion of this book may be reproduced in any form or by any process or technique without the written consent of the publisher, except for brief quotations embodied in critical articles or reviews.

Unless otherwise noted, scripture quotations are from the New Revised Standard Version of the Bible, © 1989 National Council of the Churches of Christ in the United States of America. Used by permission. All rights reserved.

This book is a collection of articles originally published for the tercentennial celebration of the Church of the Brethren in 2008. The series ran December 2007 through July 2008 in MESSENGER magazine, published by Brethren Press. Related articles on Brethren history from the May 2009 and January/February 2010 issues have also been included.

The *Dunker Guide* logo on the cover uses an artist's rendering (no photos of him exist) of Henry Kurtz, who was instrumental in the beginnings of Brethren publishing. Kurtz published several periodicals, including *The Monthly Gospel-Visiter*, the direct ancestor of today's MESSENGER. This illustration of Kurtz was drawn in 1984 by Kermon Thomasson, editor of MESSENGER 1977-1997.

Cover image: From Peter Nead's *Theological Writings on Various Subjects, or a Vindication of the Word of God* (1850); courtesy of the Brethren Historical Library and Archives (Elgin, Illinois)

Library of Congress Control Number: 2010926788
ISBN: 978-0-87178-134-5

14 13 12 11 10   1 2 3 4 5

Printed in the United States of America

CONTENTS

Foreword

Everything has a history. On the Contents page of the March 2008 issue of *Messenger*, we highlighted the magazine's own history—roots that stretch back more than 150 years. That brief summary said, in part:

"We can't look at this period of Brethren history [1808-1858] without noting one important development: the 1851 debut of *The Monthly Gospel-Visiter*, the denomination's first periodical. It was the work of Elder Henry Kurtz, a publisher and printer and something of a maverick, who became an influential figure among the Brethren."

Hopefully that was enough of a teaser to inspire at least a few people to go learn more about Kurtz, and perhaps about the magazine itself, and the rich heritage it carries. For while our vision must remain forward-looking, we can't lose sight of the path that has brought us here. Knowing where we came from helps us to know where we're going.

Much of the 300th anniversary celebration of the denomination carried the need for balance between those two worlds: How do we honor the past and allow it to shape us without being bound by it? How do we glance back over our shoulder without getting nostalgic whiplash?

Courtesy of Brethren Historical Library and Archives

When the 300th anniversary committee approached the communications and publishing staff of the church about ways to be a part of the observance, they asked *Messenger* to include some special coverage. We didn't need much convincing. A milestone of this magnitude deserved the attention of the denominational magazine. The question was how to highlight it.

At first a year-long feature emphasis through 2008 was considered, looking at blocks of 30 years each and then finishing with a forward-looking issue. That seemed a bit long to stretch out the series, especially since the anniversary's climax would come in the summer. So, instead, it was decided to examine 50 years at a time, covering six issues, plus retaining the forward-looking issue as the capstone—in the issue that would come out at the special Annual Conference in Richmond, Va.

Then content had to be decided. Brethren have always been highly relational, and we value personal stories. Rather than a general recounting of history, we decided to focus on two particular personalities in each era, trying to give some behind-the-scenes glimpses of their values and actions in narrative form. Sidebars and shorter articles would touch on other episodes of importance during that block of time.

And so it began, running from Alexander Mack Sr. and Peter Becker (1708-1758) in January on to Anna Mow and M.R. Zigler (1958-2008) in June. The final issue in July/August carried the title "Now what?" looking at 2008 and beyond.

In all, the series involved more than two dozen different men and women who wrote on subjects that spanned the globe and brought a host of unique insights and perspectives. Ken Shaffer and Logan Condon in the Brethren Historical Library and Archives were invaluable in suggesting many of these writers, as well as in digging up records and photographs from times past to build each issue.

The trail led through more dusty boxes and little-used folders and albums than one might ever think possible. Some pieces were actually handwritten by notable Brethren leaders of the past. Some explorations led to dead ends, while others brought pleasant surprises. A collection of artwork by Albert Winkler and the murals at Camp Mack in Indiana done by Medford Neher proved a treasure trove for illustration. Annual Meeting minutes and other documents shed rays of new light.

It gives one some perspective, realizing that someday curious fingers may be probing through our own records and writings and images in similar fashion. What lessons will they take from our era? What will they think of our witness?

In that forward-looking issue that capped the series, a variety of writers shared their visions and dreams for the future. One of them, McPherson (Kan.) Church of the Brethren pastor Shawn Flory Replogle (later elected 2010 Annual Conference moderator), wrote:

"I see a future for a group of believers who invites the world to join them in the journey of taking Jesus seriously, recognizing that there is a multitude of faithful responses to that effort. It is the effort of following where Jesus leads that brings us closest to being the body of Christ. And it just so happens that it offers an authenticity of faith for which this culture seems to desperately crave. The Church of the Brethren is made for this time and place."

Everything has a history, including us. What legacy will our future leave for some yet-to-be-born generation's past? In the words of a Jon Mohr song, "May all who come behind us find us faithful. . . . May the footprints that we leave lead them to believe, and the lives we live inspire them to obey."

May we be attentive to our own stories, even as we learn from those who have gone before.

—*Walt Wiltschek*

A DUNKER GUIDE TO BRETHREN HISTORY

300 years
Reclaiming the past

THE BRETHREN CELEBRATE 300 YEARS

The year 2008 marked the 300th anniversary of the Church of the Brethren and the Brethren movement that started in Schwarzenau, Germany, in 1708. Why should we care about the past?

History holds the keys

by Steve Longenecker

Remembering the Brethren past can help the present and future

George Santayana's maxim is probably every historian's favorite saying. When I taught high school, I posted it over the classroom door.

"Those who cannot remember the past are condemned to repeat it."

But Santayana leaves several points unsaid.

Most obviously, he neglects history's most appealing asset: It is fun. In brief, history is the study of everything that comprises human behavior in the past: altruism, greed, courage, cowardice, honor, sleaze, love, hatred, sex, and violence. Or, to paraphrase Ecclesiastes 3, history is birthing, dying, planting, plucking, killing, healing, breaking, building, weeping, laughing, mourning, dancing, embracing, refraining from embracing, seeking, losing, keeping, throwing away, tearing, sowing, being silent, speaking, loving, hating, making war, and making peace.

True, the players on history's stage are usually dead, but they still make up one big soap opera. If you think people are interesting, you have to like history.

> Historians use virtual time machines to share intimate moments with those from the past, and they bring the dead back to life. **They read other people's mail. No other field can say this.**

General Board file photo

Likewise, historians use their imaginations, and that's fun, too. Imagine, for example, what H. Stover Kulp, the first Brethren missionary to Nigeria, thought as he stepped off the boat. Did he feel the presence of God, or was he terrified? A Brethren family lived on the battlefield in Gettysburg, Pa., and a few months later one of them heard Lincoln's Gettysburg Address. Imagine that.

Historians enjoy themselves in other ways. They use virtual time machines to share intimate moments with those from the past, and they bring the dead back to life. They read other people's mail. No other field can say this. (That worksheet-spewing teacher you had in high school deeply misunderstood the subject.) But history is more than amusement. In fact, as Santayana suggests, it has a variety of practical and valuable uses for Brethren.

In the first place, history contributes to the core knowledge possessed by informed Brethren and thereby facilitates dialogue. Brethren conversation often includes terms like Anabaptism, Pietism, non-creedalism, Alexander Mack, John Kline, Heifer Project, and Dan West, and those who understand this vocabulary participate more fully in the exchange of ideas. Knowledge is empowering, and history contributes to that.

Second, Brethren, like everybody else, can learn from the past to improve the present. To embrace Santayana to the fullest, the heritage does more than supply terminology for sermons or Sunday school lessons. Instead, it offers practical instruction about real-life situations.

The past, for example, can help present-day Brethren comprehend the denomination's biggest current question: its dramatic loss of members. The trick is determining what from Brethren history is most informative. Did something happen in the 1960s when the decline began? The movement of Brethren into mainstream Protestantism gained speed in the '60s. Perhaps that contributed to numerical decline, because when Brethren most intently non-conformed to mainstream society, they grew. But maybe the seeds of membership loss were planted long before 1960 and only matured during this decade. A clear historical lesson on membership might be elusive, but the investigation nevertheless provides a deeper understanding of the question.

In fact, sometimes history is particularly instructive because it reflects life's messiness. Mission, for example, was important in the heritage, but its form varied, and it sends mixed signals to modern Brethren about growth. The first generation of Brethren enthusiastically spread their message as far and as wide as possible. But that quickly changed. By the middle of the 19th century Brethren evangelism was quieter, typified by John Kline. His lengthy and tiring trips into the western Virginia mountains undoubtedly won converts, but in many respects Kline simply sought to supply spiritual leadership to a region with a shortage of ministers. In the early 20th century Brethren evangelism assumed yet another shape, this time as revivals. But these fêtes of evangelism typically won the souls of Brethren children rather than capturing those outside the fold. Thus, the Brethren evangelistic heritage contains diversity. Sometimes true wisdom is the realization that life is complex, and history contributes to this.

Yet despite history's tendency to muddy the picture, occasionally it provides clarity. One constant from Brethren heritage is the refusal of Alexander Mack's spiritual descendants to hide their identity under a bushel. First-generation Brethren, Kline in the Alleghenies, and young Brethren answering an altar call all confidently embraced their Brethren-ness. Maybe the past teaches that instead of looking to evangelism for growth, which is more complicated than it sounds, Brethren today should start with a strong sense of identity. They need to know what they stand for and let it shine forth in whatever ways they feel called.

Even the past of other traditions can instruct on Brethren growth. The greatest example of religious expansion in American history was early 19th-century

Yet despite history's tendency to muddy the picture, occasionally it provides clarity. One constant from Brethren heritage is the refusal of Alexander Mack's spiritual descendants to hide their identity under a bushel.

Methodism. Within a generation or two Methodism grew from almost nothing to become the nation's largest denomination by far. Historians still strive to explain the extraordinary Methodist multiplication, but the latest attempt argues that John Wesley's movement was a product of its environment. Methodists were not smarter or better marketers than Baptists or Presbyterians, but their beliefs and organization simply fit the circumstances of the times extremely well. Early Methodism's lesson for modern Brethren, then, is that membership loss might stem from broad social trends rather than a flawed system. Perhaps neither the loss of nonconformity nor defective evangelism caused the membership drop, but the larger society simply changed, and Brethrenism now has less appeal than previously. This raises an ugly question about whether Brethren need to change core beliefs and practices to survive.

Finally, and perhaps most importantly, the heritage contributes to spiritual growth. Alexander Mack, for example, moved four times for his faith (Schriesheim, Schwarzenau, Holland, and Philadelphia). That level of commitment can stir us all. The early Brethren opposition to slavery was a bold witness that in hindsight looks prophetic, and should motivate 21st-century Brethren to stand taller for peace and justice. Climbing into the time machine helps. Imagine what it was like to participate in a love feast held by the first generation of Brethren. Maybe modern Brethren should try harder to imitate their depth of faith.

Likewise, the Brethren have a canon of historical literature, largely untapped, that is richly inspirational. Everybody has favorite sermons that when re-heard or re-read still retain power. John Kline's diary is full of helpful insights in common, everyday language that remain relevant. Dan West's emotional letter from Spain as it endured a civil war in 1937 can motivate anybody to serve his or her present age. Records from the past thus become devotional literature.

The Brethren heritage, then, is informative, which is always useful, and it offers lessons from the past—sometimes untidy, sometimes lucid—that improve the present. But most importantly, Brethren who remember their past receive nourishment for their souls and wisdom and courage for the facing of this hour.

But don't forget: It's also fun.

Why Brethren history?

by Frank Ramirez

Heritage is full of rich stories and lessons

I learned a good deal of Brethren history before I even considered joining the Brethren. What surprised me at the time was how little real Brethren knew about their own story.

In 1974, while I was a theater arts major at La Verne College in California, fellow students Mike Titus and Phil Franklin told me that professor Vernard Eller had been asked to write a play about Brethren beginnings called "A Time So Urgent." It had been commissioned for the 250th anniversary of the church in 1958 but never performed. Mike and Phil got this crazy idea that we ought to take this play out into Brethren society that summer. Could I help?

It was the height of the gas crisis, with long lines at the pump, but the college was offering us a van (wonderfully refurbished because the staff mistakenly thought it was for the president) and a gas card. We would depend on Brethren churches for food, lodging, and maybe an offering or two.

So it was that I learned about Alexander Mack and Pietism and Anabaptists and the Treaty of Westphalia and Hochmann von Hochenau, from the play and from reading Don Durnbaugh's *European Origins of the Brethren*. After 78 days, 15,000 miles, 50 Brethren congregations (from California and Washington through Virginia, Maryland, West Virginia, Pennsylvania, Ohio, Indiana, and Illinois and back again), Annual Conference, Brethren campgrounds, all six Brethren colleges, and a visit to Bethany Theological Seminary, as well as a stop at National Youth Conference, I not only knew about the Brethren in 1708, I saw for myself what the Brethren looked like 266 years later. And I liked what I saw.

Why Brethren history? I know some people ask that, arms akimbo, leaning back in their chairs with a skeptical look as they ask, "Isn't it more important to be Christian than Brethren?" But if we knew our Brethren history better, we'd

Courtesy of Brethren Historical Library and Archives

know that to be Christian *is* to be Brethren. Do not forget—the intent of the first Brethren was not to create a new church, but restore the original one.

This is our family story. It helps to know why we are who we are, which red flags turn our faces pink, and why every conception of Brethren heaven probably includes sweet pie and hot coffee. More important: Brethren history is fun.

There's the shark that's pulled on deck chomping and snapping while John Naas makes the dangerous crossing to America. There's the accidental speech made by Don Murray about Brethren Volunteer Service when vice presidential candidate C. Estes Kefauver was late that led Sen. Hubert Humphrey to lobby for a Peace Corps, or Evelyn Trostle holding her ground in front of the orphanage during the Armenian genocide. There's the venerably crippled Julia Gilbert speaking on the floor of Annual Conference and changing the way we share communion, a newspaper report from 1877 that made it clear that the Brethren love feast was really a three-day slumber party, and John Lewis leaping from his horse to save Mark Twain's sister-in-law and her companions from certain death on a runaway horse cart. There's the story of how one of the most infamous murderers of all time operated the X-ray equipment at the Brethren hospital in Castañer in Puerto Rico. There's interviewing Clarence Quay, who was a smoke jumper during World War II, or Abraham Harley Cassell (with his six weeks of schooling) collecting more books than just about anyone else ever and saving Brethren history in the process. There's P.R. Wrightsman riding his horse through the middle of a threatening band of Confederate soldiers because it was time to cook love feast, and even the threat of death wasn't enough to scare Brethren away from the

This is our family story. It helps to know why we are who we are, which red flags turn our faces pink, and why every conception of Brethren heaven probably includes sweet pie and hot coffee. **More important: Brethren history is fun.**

smells of beef and broth; Helena Kruger sneaking refugees out of the Soviet zone in her car while working in Europe; Dan West coming to the realization that what these hungry people need is not a cup but a cow; shaking hands with Carlisle Frederick, one of the Brethren involved in the famous Starvation Experiment. . . .

Once we know a little about our history we learn that we have always been on the move, that our Bibles have always been open, and that we're still learning and growing. It's always been that way. We've never been frozen in time.

Why Brethren history? How can we possibly know who we are if we're content to let others define us by the way we practice the faith instead of reflecting why our spiritual ancestors made their biblical choices? History, after all, isn't about the frozen past. History helps us to understand the future long before it happens, it frees us from our misconceptions ("Alexander Mack would be spinning in his grave if he knew . . ."), and sometimes it just entertains!

Two other thoughts: First, just as knowing medical history can be crucial in terms of prevention and health maintenance, so, too, it doesn't hurt for us to know who we were and how we got here. Read Steve Longenecker's *The Brethren in the Age of World War* or Carl Bowman's classic *Brethren Society* and you'll discover there's nothing new about today's controversies. Second, in the biblical book of Revelation it's clear that the communion of saints includes both the living and breathing believers as well as those who have gone on to their reward. They are part of one body. So are we—and our living saints ought to know more about the essential connection with our spiritual ancestors.

The 300th anniversary of the first Brethren baptism is a great time to remember, re-learn, or just plain learn about our history and heritage—not as relics of a dead past, but as companions in our continuing pledge to follow in the footsteps of Jesus.

The keepers of history

by Kenneth M. Shaffer Jr. and Logan Condon

Archives provide significant service of preservation

What becomes of a congregation's membership records and council meeting minutes when the congregation is disorganized? Are the records destroyed? Does the last pastor to serve the congregation keep the records? Are they stored at the district office?

According to the Church of the Brethren polity manual, congregational records become the property of the district, and the district decides where to deposit the records. Typically districts place congregational records at one of the Brethren archives. These records generally include newsletters, bulletins, directories, yearly budgets, annual reports, etc., as well as minutes and membership records. Some congregations transfer their inactive records directly to the district-approved archives on a periodic basis. And districts sometimes place their inactive records at the archives they have selected.

So what is an archives? An archives collects, organizes, and preserves materials. A Brethren archives typically collects, organizes, and preserves Brethren materials such as congregational and district records; Brethren pub-

> **Archives are the major preservers of Brethren history.** They maintain materials that enable historians to write accurate histories. But archives also are used by elected Brethren leaders, by the staff of Brethren institutions, by genealogists, and by people seeking information about Brethren beliefs and practices.

Archivist Ken Shaffer cares for materials in the Brethren Historical Library and Archives in Elgin, Ill.

lications; Brethren dissertations and theses; the diaries, correspondence, and personal papers of Brethren leaders; Brethren genealogies; photographs and other images; and sometimes artifacts.

Archives are the major preservers of Brethren history. They maintain materials that enable historians to write accurate histories. But archives also are used by elected Brethren leaders, by the staff of Brethren institutions, by genealogists, and by people seeking information about Brethren beliefs and practices. Archives help Brethren understand who they are today in light of their past, and help non-Brethren better know the Brethren.

One reason for the existence of several archives in the Church of the Brethren is that districts have the authority to determine where to deposit their records. Often districts decide to place their records at the Brethren-related college in their area. For example, the archives at Manchester College (North Manchester, Ind.) is the repository for the districts in Indiana.

The Brethren Historical Library and Archives (BHLA) in Illinois is designated as the repository for Annual Conference records and the records of Annual Conference agencies. Some districts have designated BHLA as their official archives. BHLA also has the records of several Brethren associations, the personal papers of Brethren leaders such as Dan West, and a large collection of photographs.

Bethany Theological Seminary is served by the Earlham College Libraries in Richmond, Ind. They maintain a collection of Church of the Brethren books, periodicals, and pamphlets. Also at Earlham are the Bethany-owned Huston Bibles Collection and a significant portion of the Cassel Collection.

The Young Center for Anabaptist and Pietist Studies located on the campus of Elizabethtown (Pa.) College maintains a significant collection of Brethren materials, including materials from the Ephrata Cloister. As their names states, they also collect other Pietist and Anabaptist materials.

The Brethren Heritage Center in Brookville, Ohio, is the repository for Southern Ohio District. The center also collects the materials of other Brethren groups that trace their origins to Schwarzenau in 1708.

Some other Brethren groups also maintain their own libraries and archives. The Brethren Church Archives, which is under the direction of Ashland (Ohio) University, collects the materials of the Brethren Church. The Morgan Library, which serves Grace College and Grace Theological Seminary in Winona Lake, Ind., collects the materials of the Fellowship of Grace Brethren Churches and the materials of the Conservative Grace Brethren Churches.

A large block in the aptly named Alexander Mack Memorial Library at Bridgewater (Va.) College tells about the founder of the Church of the Brethren.

The Young Center

The Young Center for Anabaptist and Pietist Studies, located on the campus of Elizabethtown (Pa.) College, holds a unique place in academia. It is the only national institute for research in this specific field, and it has received high marks for its work.

In 2004 its efforts were rewarded with a $500,000 "challenge grant" from the National Endowment for the Humanities, which required a 4:1 match by the end of January 2008. The resulting $2.5 million endowment created a faculty chair position in Anabaptist and Pietist studies, supported and enhanced existing programs, and expanded the center's collection.

The center offers a variety of lectures, exhibits, and other programs, many of them open to the public. The building contains several display areas, a bookshop, a reading room, and the Bucher Meetinghouse. Jeff Bach, formerly on the faculty of Bethany Theological Seminary, began as the new director of the Young Center in 2007.

More details on the Young Center can be found at www.etown.edu/YoungCenter.aspx.

Courtesy of Elizabethtown College

Donald B. Kraybill, former director and current senior fellow at the Young Center, is nationally recognized for his research and writing.

A DUNKER GUIDE TO BRETHREN HISTORY

1708-1758
The Brethren begin

Nevin Dulabaum

From 1708 to 1758: The initial years of Brethren history were times of energy and difficulties, transition and travels. Alexander Mack (Sr.) and Peter Becker stood among the key leaders who guided the early Brethren through this exciting and turbulent period, moving from Germany's Palatinate region to the Germantown area outside Philadelphia.

Alexander Mack
A seeker of scripture

by Alice Archer

Organizational and unity-building skills gave new movement a foundation

Alexander Mack was born in 1679 in a family of village leaders in Schriesheim, Germany. His father was twice mayor. During Mack's childhood years his family fled three times into nearby hills for safety from invading armies, returning to help rebuild life in the community.

When his oldest brother died, Mack's parents expected him to partner with another brother in the family mill, ending any plans for a university education. Mack's marriage to Anna Margaret Kling in 1701 united two of the leading families of Schriesheim.

Mack soon became disillusioned with the local Reformed Church and joined the Pietist movement. While some Pietists continued a relationship with local congregations, others known as Separatists withdrew from organized religion. Mack became a Separatist. In violation of laws against private religious gatherings, he began a Bible study and prayer group. In 1706 he invited Ernst Christoph Hochmann von Hochenau, a radical Pietist and charismatic preacher, to the mill. Officials broke up the meeting threatening to have them arrested. The Mack family, making a hasty decision to flee, soon found refuge in the village of Schwarzenau.

They perceived themselves not as a new church or denomination but rather a part of the church established by Jesus himself. **The New Testament church became their model for organization.**

Medford D. Neher / Courtesy of Camp Mack

There Mack shared a sizable inheritance from his father with other refugees. Still in his 20s, he was looked to as a natural leader, respected for his knowledge of and ability to interpret the Bible. Already familiar with Mennonites whom he had visited in "heartfelt love," he emphasized the New Testament, especially the Gospels.

His writings demonstrate diligent study of the Bible as well as sources from church history. Baptism became a major issue. Mack notes in his writing that John the Baptist always baptized where water was plentiful. He also found support in early church history for immersion. While familiar with English Baptists who immersed once backward and Dutch Collegiants who immersed once forward, his small group in Schwarzenzau came to a unified conclusion. Baptism should be by immersing three times forward in the "name of the Father, and of the Son, and of the Holy Spirit," words still familiar to Brethren baptism today.

In 1707, Mack traveled with Hochmann as far as Switzerland to encourage the Pietists. When Hochmann was arrested and imprisoned, the Pietists in Schwarzenau looked to Mack for leadership.

The New Testament church became their model for a disciplined community as they experimented with a variety of practices, abandoning some that Mack referred to later as "errors."

Encouraged by two "foreign visitors," most likely Dutch Collegiants, Mack and another Pietist wrote Hochmann for counsel concerning baptism. Hochmann's words of counsel included an admonition to "count the cost."

Then, in August 1708, Alexander Mack, his wife Anna Margaret, Andrew and Joanna Boni, George Grebe, John and Johanna Kipping, and Lucas Vetter gathered on the bank of the Eder River. Not wanting any one person identified as founder, the group cast lots with the understanding that the name of the one chosen would never be revealed. The one so chosen baptized Mack. Mack then baptized the other seven.

By that act a new group had been formed: the "New Baptists" or "Schwarzenau Baptists" as they called themselves. After prayers and singing they dispersed, aware that in most German states they could have been levied heavy fines, imprisoned, or exiled. They perceived themselves not as a new church or denomination but rather a part of the church established by Jesus himself. The New Testament church became their model for organization. They initiated the love feast to re-enact the last supper of Jesus with his apostles.

Both Pietist and Anabaptist ideals became integrated into their theology. The New Testament prevailed over the Old in matters of ethical and spiritual life, including ideals of no force in religion and non-participation of Christians in war. But underlying all the specific principles, Mack's writings return over and over again to his commitment to be obedient to Christ.

The love feast, Mack argued, should be limited to those who had "counted the cost" in separating themselves from the world and committing themselves to live in obedience to Christ. Even within his lifetime this view of the love feast became a point of contention with those who favored a more inclusive perspective.

From Schwarzenau Mack traveled to the Marienborn area, preaching and performing baptisms—an illegal action. By 1715 persecution caused most of the Marienborn congregation to flee to Schwarzenau or Krefeld. By 1720 the Schwarzenau group had grown to about 200. The region's ruler, Count Henry, described them as inoffensive and having a pure desire to lead lives pleasing to God. His daughter called them quiet people who spent time in Bible study and deeds of kindness.

Under Peter Becker's leadership, many of the Krefeld congregation had emigrated to Pennsylvania in 1719. Those in Schwarzenau came to be threatened with persecution, so in 1720 the Schwarzenau congregation moved to Surhuisterveen in north Holland, where Mennonites welcomed them and helped them resettle. There Mack's wife died unexpectedly, then also his young daughter Christina.

Employment was soon threatened as the peat fields of Surhuisterveen became depleted, so they decided to follow Becker's group to the New World. With help from the Collegiants and Mennonites Mack led about 100 to Rotterdam in 1729, where they set sail for Philadelphia. Their ship was small for ocean travel, and their captain had never ventured across the Atlantic.

The Germantown congregation established by the Krefeld group eagerly welcomed the new immigrants and Mack as minister. The economic opportunities

MACK IS BACK

Alexander Mack has enjoyed a resurgence of sorts with the appearance of "A-Mack." Mack, portrayed with a mix of whimsy and reverence by Larry Glick of Shenandoah District, has made appearances at National Youth Conference, National Older Adult Conference, and other events. He has also appeared in some video spots and has his own Facebook page.

and religious freedom of Pennsylvania were a blessing after the hardships in Europe. Their enthusiastic, evangelistic efforts soon led to the development of several new congregations.

Mack died on February 19, 1735, at his home in Germantown and was buried in a community cemetery. A humble man, he did not want his grave marked and only reluctantly agreed to a small slab at the insistence of his sons. In 1894 his remains were moved to the cemetery behind the Germantown church.

Alexander Mack wrote little about himself, nor did he seek personal honor. Others have written little about him. Yet today, 300 years later, a street in Schriesheim and a former school in Schwarzenau are named for him. Across the Atlantic a college library (in Bridgewater, Va.) and a camp (Camp Alexander Mack in Milford, Ind.) bear his name. Several denominations look to Mack as a founder of their faith—a title he did not want.

What makes Alexander Mack so memorable? Perhaps the early years of observing his parents' community-rebuilding efforts imprinted good organizational skills on him. In an age of much "do your own thing" spirituality, his quiet organizing set a solid foundation for the "brethren" movement. Today these denominations, along with the Community of True Inspiration—popularly known as the Amana Colonies in Iowa—continue as visible reminders of the German Pietist movement.

Neither a charismatic leader nor a powerful preacher, his gift was gathering with others for intense study of the scriptures and guiding the group into a unity of spirit. Alexander Mack's spiritual quest was for a "heart-felt faith" lived in obedience to Christ. The results of that faith would be seen by the fruits it produced. Asked "And how shall the Brethren be known?" he is said to have replied, "By the manner of their living."

1708-1758

Peter Becker
Forgotten founder

by James Benedict

Quiet leader guided Brethren through bumpy early years in America

Overshadowed in his own time and largely overlooked since, Peter Becker provided humble but persistent leadership that enabled the first Brethren in America to form a congregation and flourish.

Becker was deeply involved in promoting meetings among the scattered Brethren in 1722 and 1723. Several of the meetings were even held in Becker's home. It was Becker who was chosen to perform the first baptisms in Germantown and to lead the first love feast. And it was Becker who encouraged and participated in the evangelistic work that led to the formation of the second and third Brethren congregations in America. Yet in spite of his great contributions to the

Medford D. Neher / Courtesy of Camp Mack

> Mack and Beissel far outshone him as preachers, writers, and influential figures. But Becker was recognized for his sincerity, common sense, care for others, and patience. **These qualities made Becker the perfect person to lead the Brethren through the turbulent first decades in America.**

founding of the church in America, Peter Becker is little more than a name to most Brethren today. He deserves better.

Becker was born in the village of Dudelsheim, northeast of Frankfurt, Germany, in 1687. Baptized into the Reformed church, he grew up to become a prosperous farmer with extensive landholdings. Yet he also grew dissatisfied with the established church. He became interested in the enthusiasm and deep spirituality of the radical Pietist movement. He was especially attracted to the preaching and teaching of the radical Pietist leader Hochmann von Hochenau. Hochmann's influence prepared Becker to hear and respond to the message of Brethren minister Johannes Naas, who visited the Dudelsheim area in 1714. Peter Becker and his wife, Anna Dorothea, were baptized by Naas on the 15th of May, 1714.

Dudelsheim was located in the Marienborn region, which had been an area of religious toleration for several years. The counts who ruled the area welcomed religious dissenters for economic reasons, but urged them not to cause trouble. Shortly before Becker was baptized, the Community of True Inspiration—another radical Pietist group—formed in the area and began to provoke the civil authorities. The Inspirationists believed they were receiving direct messages from God, including scathing denunciations and warnings directed at non-Pietist clergy and government officials. This stirred up animosity toward all radical Pietists in the area.

The baptism of the Beckers proved to be the straw that broke the camel's back. Previous baptisms had only involved refugees in the area; the Beckers were natives and citizens. Seeking to stop the spread of radical Pietism before it got completely out of hand, Count Karl August (the ruler of Marienborn) gave the Brethren and others a choice: Practice your religion only in your own homes or leave. The Brethren, including the Beckers, elected to leave.

Peter and Anna Dorothea sold their land and moved with other Brethren to the city of Krefeld. There, Peter made a living as a weaver while helping to give leadership to the Krefeld congregation. Becker, Johannes Naas, Christian Liebe, and Stephen Koch were leaders who guided the group, which flourished at first. But Krefeld was also home to Mennonites, and a crisis arose in the Brethren congregation over intermarriage. Although the Brethren and Mennonites were similar in many ways, they also had differences—notably the mode of baptism and different attitudes toward the emotionalism associated with radical Pietism. The disagreement about the permissibility of intermarriage led to a great deal of rancor and eventually a split among the Brethren.

The experience shook Peter Becker and several other Brethren deeply. They elected to leave the area, boarded a ship, and settled near Philadelphia in 1719. Notably, they did not immediately re-form as a congregation. Some families lived near Germantown, which was originally established by Mennonites who had left Krefeld in 1683. Others scattered to the north and west.

It wasn't until 1722 that Peter Becker and a few others organized the meetings that brought the Brethren back together. Discussions continued for some time, but when six candidates requested baptism, the Brethren took the formal step of naming Becker their minister. He performed the baptism and administered the first love feast on American soil.

Soon thereafter Becker and 13 other men undertook an evangelistic trip into the outlying areas, forming congregations in the Coventry area (near what is now Pottstown, Pa.) and in Conestoga (further west toward Lancaster). Each of these congregations, along with the original group in Germantown, grew. Eighteen years after their beginning at Schwarzenau, Germany, the Brethren were flourishing in America. But another bitter split was on the horizon.

Within a year or two of arriving in America, Peter Becker had developed a good business again as a weaver. He welcomed a young, unaffiliated radical Pietist by the name of J. Conrad Beissel as an apprentice. Beissel had spent some time in Germany as part of the Community of True Inspiration but emigrated alone. Becker eventually talked Beissel into becoming a member of the Brethren, and baptized Beissel in 1724. Then the usually cautious and thoughtful Becker did something out of character: He appointed Beissel the minister of the Conestoga congregation.

Beissel proved to be more of a mystic and more of an authoritarian leader than many Brethren were ready to accept. Though immensely creative and gift-

DID YOU KNOW?

One of the few (and perhaps the only) Brethren institution to bear Peter Becker's name is the Peter Becker Community, a retirement home located in Harleysville, Pa. (www.peterbeckercommunity.com). Camp Alexander Mack, in Milford, Ind., has a Peter Becker Lodge on its campus.

ed with charisma, Beissel lacked tact. He alienated many Brethren, split the Conestoga congregation, and eventually repudiated his Brethren baptism. Becker, as leader of the mother congregation at Germantown, did his best to deal with the conflict, but many Brethren left to join Beissel at Ephrata.

In 1729, Peter Becker and the other Brethren in America were joined by a second wave of Brethren immigrants, including Alexander Mack. Mack was the unquestioned leader among the Brethren in Europe, and Becker graciously—and perhaps with great relief— deferred to him. Mack attempted to repair the split with Beissel. Becker supported Mack in his efforts, but reconciliation did not take place.

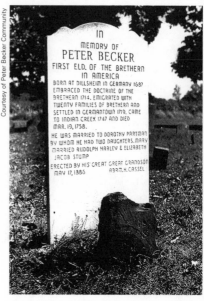

Courtesy of Peter Becker Community

In
MEMORY OF
PETER BECKER
FIRST ELD. OF THE BRETHREN
IN AMERICA
BORN AT DILLSHEIM IN GERMANY 1687
EMBRACED THE DOCTRINE OF THE
BRETHERN 1714. EMIGRATED WITH
TWENTY FAMILIES OF BRETHERN AND
SETTLED IN GERMANTOWN 1719. CAME
TO INDIAN CREEK 1747 AND DIED
MAR. 19, 1758.
HE WAS MARRIED TO DOROTHY PARTMAN
BY WHOM HE HAD TWO DAUGHTERS, MARY
MARRIED RUDOLPH HARLEY & ELIZABETH
JACOB STUMP
ERECTED BY HIS GREAT GREAT GRANDSON
MAY 17, 1886   ABRM. H. CASSEL

A newer gravestone stands over Peter Becker's original simple marker in Harleysville, Pa.

When Mack died six years later, Peter Becker again stepped forward into the leadership of the Brethren in America. Unfortunately, the troubles with Beissel continued, and Becker watched in disappointment as another large contingent of Brethren departed in 1739 to join Beissel's Ephrata Community. Peter Becker continued his humble and caring leadership of those who remained.

In 1747, Peter Becker and his wife moved to a three-acre tract near Skippack, where one of their daughters lived. Active in the Indian Creek congregation till his death in 1758, Becker was buried in the cemetery of the Klein meetinghouse near Harleysville, Pa. Over a century later, Brethren historian and Becker descendant Abraham H. Cassel arranged for a large memorial gravestone to be placed on Peter Becker's grave.

Peter Becker himself had requested only a small, simple marker with his initials and date of death. Somehow, that fits the man better than any monument. He lacked both the personality and the inclination to promote himself. Mack and Beissel far outshone him as preachers, writers, and influential figures. But Becker was recognized for his sincerity, common sense, care for others, and patience. These qualities made Becker the perfect person to lead the Brethren through the turbulent first decades in America.

Schwarzenau
Then and now

by Nevin Dulabaum

As I leaned over, I dipped my hand into the cool, flowing waters of the Eder River. Mist hung in the air that August morning, limiting visibility to about a quarter-mile as I turned around and looked toward the base of the hill that leads to the Hüttental (Valley of the Huts), site of Alexander and Anna Mack's home in Schwarzenau, Germany. I imagined the Macks and six others—five men and three women—making their way down the hill, descending through the mist and continuing straight to the water.

Standing by the Eder, one easily can imagine the first eight Brethren rebaptizing themselves in August 1708 in open defiance of the Catholic, Reformed, and Lutheran churches. For although the world has changed in many ways since that year, in a way Schwarzenau feels as though little has changed.

Sure, modernization has come to the town, but development and expansion on the village's boundaries has been so slight that Schwarzenau is a living snapshot of the early 18th century. There aren't developments that have consumed the ground where the first Brethren walked; there's ground! The Eder continues to flow past open fields, and one can walk freely along the water's edge.

The town, which celebrated its 950th anniversary the year after the Brethren celebrated their 300th, has never had more than 1,000 residents living in it at one

> . . . Schwarzenau is a living snapshot of the early 18th century. There aren't developments that have consumed the ground where the first Brethren walked; there's ground! **The Eder continues to flow past open fields, and one can walk freely along the water's edge.**

time. It is in a largely rural area of northern Germany—an area of rolling hills, thick forests, and meandering roads; a land where farming and the harvesting of timber are two primary vocations.

In the center of Schwarzenau, on the southwest side of the river, are about half of the village's houses, the school, and the timber mill. This half of the village is flat, as it is on the river valley floor. Along one of the streets is a sign that shows the village map, states that Schwarzenau has existed since 1059, and acknowledges the village as the birthplace of the Brethren movement.

A short walk to the south leads to the Renno Guesthouse, which has hosted numerous tour groups through the years and has the guest books filled with the names of countless traveling Brethren to prove it.

Across the Eder and close to the village's one bridge is the Herrenhaus, the manor house, which was built in 1650. From 1698 to 1723, it was home to

Heinrich Albrecht, who allowed religious dissenters like the Brethren to take refuge in his community.

Nevin Dulabaum

Most of the houses on this side of the river, the northeast side, are on the side of the hill that forms one edge of the valley. Travelers going up the hill pass a medieval tower, the now-closed school that the General Board helped finance in the 1950s, the cemetery, and then enter an area of timber that rises up over the village. Continuing northwest for a short distance, travelers find themselves at the Hüttental, an area of Schwarzenau that is higher and separated by a forest from the town proper. Here lies the long row house (seen above) where Alexander and Anna Mack purportedly lived.

Two of the five units now comprise the Alexander Mack Museum. Two of the other units are apartments, and one, at the far end, is a stable.

The museum pays tribute to Mack and the Brethren movement, with one room decorated with 18th-century furnishings. There are other Brethren literature, photos, maps, a replica of the ship Mack and others sailed on to North America, mannequins dressed in traditional German Baptist Brethren garb, and commemorative items, such as a framed document from the 1950s that honors the 250th anniversary of the church. The museum also holds Schwarzenau artifacts, including a banner from the early 1900s and a framed tribute to an American space shuttle astronaut who had distant ties to the village.

Walking out of the museum and slightly down the hill, one can see the Eder River in the distance, winding its way to downtown Schwarzenau, which is slightly around a hill and to the left. Of all the Schwarzenau landmarks, it is the river that is the most striking from the time when the Brethren resided here. Its pristine water, soothing sound, and cool feel all hark back to a day when eight Brethren took a bold, daring step that became a movement and brought the witness for peace and justice and compassion to the world. It is a symbol of Christ. It is a memory of the Brethren.

That is why on that August morning when I lowered my hand into the Eder, I filled a bottle with the precious liquid that I still have to this day.

1708-1758

John Naas
Tall man or tall tale?
by Frank Ramirez

Will the real John Naas (1669-1741) please stand up?
Was he the character in the Dorothy Brandt Davis children's book *The Tall Man* who endured torture cheerfully because he had no captain but Immanuel?

Maybe not. This most famous story about Naas may not be true. According to an account more than a century and a half later by Abraham Harley Cassel, Naas—"a man of great physique and commanding personality"—was press-ganged to become part of the royal bodyguard for the king of Prussia. Despite excruciating tortures, including thumbscrews and being forced to hang by a toe and a thumb, Naas did not submit. When finally dragged before the throne he was reported to have said that he had no captain but Christ, which so impressed the king that he was released and given a gold coin for his faithfulness.

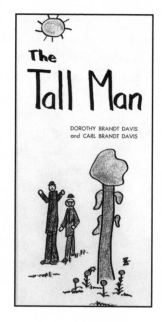

There is no such account among either the European or Colonial documents, although Naas is often mentioned in many other regards. It is possible that some confused him with John Fisher from Hall, who was tortured for 10 days and, after refusing to renounce his faith, pricked with pins all over his body and thrown into a hole, where he was found by a prince who took pity on him and arranged for his release.

Then again, it is quite likely that several Brethren, including both Fisher and Naas, were tortured for their faith. One reason the story was unknown until Cassel printed it in an 1871 arti-

> When finally dragged before the throne he was reported to have said that **he had no captain but Christ,** which so impressed the king that he was released and given a gold coin for his faithfulness.

cle might be that Brethren didn't brag. And victims don't choose to relive horrors. And, as the Baptist Colonial era historian Morgan Edwards wrote regarding Naas: "I am sorry I could not come at more of this good man's history (for these people keep no records), and all his contemporaries are dead."

One of my favorite stories about Naas, told years later by Alexander Mack Jr., was about a sick woman who earnestly desired to be baptized over the objections of her friends who feared the immersion would kill her. Naas asked the sick woman, "Do you have faith that this work of the Lord can be carried out on your sick body?" When she answered yes he said, "Then I also have faith to perform it on you." She came out of the baptismal waters healed in body as well as spirit.

Naas' most striking legacy, however, is his lengthy letter describing his 1733 voyage to Pennsylvania including cramped and smoky quarters, constant diarrhea and vomiting, horrendous food, and many deaths. However the author's faith in God never wavered even when he was paralyzed for two weeks after a ladder caused him to crash below decks. The vivid description of the crew landing a live shark on deck and the wonder of the first fresh fruit after a long voyage caused it to be reprinted on several occasions.

Despite his distress over church conflicts he remained loyal to the Brethren, serving the Amwell congregation of New Jersey. Next time you sing "Savior of my soul" (*Hymnal: A Worship Book* 549), think of its author, John Naas, and his faithful service to the Brethren on two continents.

A DUNKER GUIDE TO BRETHREN HISTORY

1758-1808
New steps in a new world

Glenn R. Riegel

From 1758 to 1808: Brethren activity centered in southeastern Pennsylvania over the last half of the 18th century, from the growing church at Germantown led by Alexander Mack Jr. and Christopher Sauer to evangelistic mission journeys into the lands beyond. Bit by bit, Brethren built their identity in the "New World."

Christopher Sauer Jr.
Faith under fire
by Kenneth M. Shaffer Jr.

**Influential printer lost everything
during the Revolutionary War**

O n the night of May 24, 1778, Christopher Sauer Jr., a Brethren minister and printer, was forced from his home in Germantown, Pa., by a party of American soldiers. He was marched through cornfields and when he—being nearly 57 years old—could not keep up with the young soldiers in the dark, he was prodded in the back with bayonets.

The next morning he was forced to remove all his clothes and given pants and a shirt that were so full of holes that they barely covered his body. Then his hair and beard were cut and he was painted red and black, the colors of the British, to show he was loyal to the king and a traitor to the American Revolution. Next Sauer was forced to march barefoot to the American camp where he learned he was accused of being "an oppressor of the righteous and a spy." With the help of Gen. Peter Muhlenberg, the son of a Lutheran pastor who knew Sauer, he was eventually released, but not permitted to return to his home in Germantown.

Unfortunately this was not the end of Sauer's persecution. He was declared a

Christopher Sauer Jr. was a well-to-do man who lost everything during the revolution, in part because of his religious beliefs. **However, he did not lose the respect and love of the Brethren.**

For The Glory of God and My Neighbors' Good

Albert Winkler / Courtesy of BHLA

traitor, and two months later all of his property and possessions were confiscated and sold by the revolutionary government, including his printing equipment and household goods. Even his medicines were sold. Sauer spent the remaining six years of his life working as a bookbinder to help support his younger children and to repay the loans given to him by friends when he was dispossessed.

Before the American Revolution, Christopher Sauer Jr. had presided over the influential Sauer Press, which had been founded by his father. He inherited the press in 1758 when his father died. Under Sauer Jr., the press published two editions (1763 and 1776) of the famous Sauer Bible. He also continued publishing the newspaper and almanac begun by his father. In 1764 he began publishing a religious periodical that he distributed free to those who subscribed to his other

> **When the revolution began, Sauer and the Brethren were caught in a dilemma. To whom did they owe their allegiance—the English king or the Pennsylvania Assembly that supported the revolution?**

publications. This periodical is thought to be the first of a religious nature published in America.

Sauer was born in Germany in 1721 and immigrated to colonial Pennsylvania with his parents in 1724. There is no record that his father was Brethren, and his mother became a follower of Conrad Beissel and lived at the Ephrata Cloister for more than 12 years. But Sauer joined the Germantown congregation when he was 15, was elected to the ministry at 26, and ordained at age 31. He and Alexander Mack Jr. were good friends, and both were ordained on the same day. Sauer married Catherine Scharpnack in 1751, and Mack Jr. officiated at the ceremony.

When the revolution began, Sauer and the Brethren were caught in a dilemma. To whom did they owe their allegiance—the English king or the Pennsylvania Assembly that supported the revolution? According to Romans 13:1, they were called to "be subject to the governing authorities"; but to whom or what had God given the authority? In general, Brethren preferred to remain neutral. The Pennsylvania Assembly, however, wanted to force citizens to take a stand and instituted the "test act," which required white males to swear allegiance to the state of Pennsylvania and renounce the king.

During the summer of 1778, the test act was harshly enforced in parts of Pennsylvania. This no doubt explains in part the persecution of Sauer during that summer, since he refused to take the oath. But there were other factors. First, two of Sauer's sons definitely supported the British during the revolution, and Sauer had lived with one of his sons in Philadelphia when it was held by the British. Second, Sauer was an influential leader among German-speaking citizens; and the revolutionaries wanted to make an example of him. Third, Sauer was a pacifist and refused to voluntarily support the war. When required to pay taxes to support the war, he said the money was for poor women and children.

Christopher Sauer Jr. was a well-to-do man who lost everything during the revolution, in part because of his religious beliefs. However, he did not lose the respect and love of the Brethren. He continued to serve as a pastor and visited congregations to preach and ordain deacons and ministers. Even though he lost his wealth and influence, he continued to live according to the motto that is said to have hung in his print shop: "To the glory of God and my neighbor's good."

Sources: *The Brethren in Colonial America,* edited by Donald F. Durnbaugh; *The Christopher Sauers,* by Stephen L. Longenecker; *Conscience in Crisis,* by Richard K. MacMaster and others; *The Brethren Encyclopedia,* pp. 1145-1146.

AIDED BY A FRIEND

While being forced to march barefoot by the American soldiers, Sauer was given a pair of shoes by a friend. Concerning the incident, Sauer writes: "A friend of mine seeing me in that condition asked them whether they would take the shoes from me if he would give me a pair. The officer gave his word they should not be taken from me if he would give me a pair, and so he took the shoes from his feet and the hat from his head and gave them to me, but after we had marched six miles a soldier came and demanded my shoes and took them and gave me his old slabs which wounded my feet very much." —from *The Brethren in Colonial America,* edited by Donald F. Durnbaugh, p. 402.

Alexander Mack Jr.
The tolerant reconciler
by Frank Ramirez

**'Sander' Mack led Brethren for more
than half a century**

The story is told that Floyd Mallott, who taught Brethren history at Bethany many decades ago, used to write on the blackboard the dates during which the old Dunkers in Europe decided they needed to practice celibacy. He would then write down the year Alexander Mack Jr. was born to Anna Margaretha Kling Mack and Alexander Mack Sr., two of the original eight.

The birth year fell smack dab in the middle of the celibate period.

The Brethren experiment in celibacy was only temporary. Our ancestors in the faith returned to the scriptures and decided it was not a biblical practice. And while some might chuckle at this proof that Brethren occasionally found out the hard way that a particular biblical interpretation was impractical, to my mind it is symbolic of the way Mack Jr. (or "Sander" Mack as he was generally known all his long life), bridged the gap between idealism and realism, perfect practice and practicality.

During the tercentennial year I heard a lot of references to the senior Mack, with good reason. He was a leader of the Brethren in Europe and our first min-

The arc of his life story, which included loss, alienation, depression, and restoration, **helped the Brethren remain strong in Colonial America** as well as the new nation because he helped model forgiveness and reconciliation.

Medford D. Neher / Courtesy of Camp Mack

Alexander Mack Jr. and Colonial printer Christopher Sauer II were co-pastors of the Germantown congregation.

ister. But for my money the reason the Brethren experiment is still going strong has a lot more to do with Junior. The arc of his life story, which included loss, alienation, depression, and restoration, helped the Brethren remain strong in Colonial America as well as the new nation because he helped model forgiveness and reconciliation. Sander Mack is the patron saint for all of us who are muddling through, who recognize that Jesus Christ is the perfect Lord and the rest of us are just waiting to be perfected.

The early Brethren instituted the ban as part of their understanding of Matthew 18, in order to provide a mechanism for reconciliation. But Mack Sr., who was held in high regard by his contemporaries, may not have been as successful at this as some. There is a record of a harsh outburst directed by the elder Mack at his mentor Hochmann von Hochenau—who himself turned away wrath with gentle words to the effect that when they greeted each other in heaven none of this would matter. The Brethren in Krefeld actually split over the issue of whether one could marry outside the faith. Evidently the senior Mack was unable to reconcile the parties, one group of which then sailed for Pennsylvania in 1719. When the Mack family followed a decade later it was hoped that the patriarch of the family would be able to heal the rift caused by Conrad Beissel, who founded a cloister in Ephrata and split many Brethren families as some chose to follow him into a celibate lifestyle. However, the description of Mack's encounter with Beissel makes it clear he was unsuccessful. Far from healing the breach, their meeting—contentious to say the least—broadened the divide.

By contrast, Sander Mack had a tremendous influence as a moderating reconciler, a caregiver, and an advocate for the poor and dispossessed. Far from one to draw strict denominational lines, he continued to list individuals as a brother or sister even if they left the fellowship. All of this, combined with the twists and turns of his long life and varied experiences (he earned his living as a weaver), contributed to and enhanced his reputation for moderation.

Born in Europe in 1712, he suffered the loss of his mother and a sister when he was only 8 years old, while the Mack family struggled to survive as religious refugees. Baptized in 1728, he migrated to Pennsylvania with his father a year later.

Sander left the Brethren for about 12 years following his father's death, overcome by depression, and ironically took up residence for a decade at the cloister under the guidance of his father's adversary, Conrad Beissel. Over time, however, Sander became disillusioned with Beissel's authoritarian ways. After he left the cloister he traveled a great distance on foot with a few friends to set up a spiritual camp on the frontier in western Virginia. But life as a religious hermit proved a failure, and after a warning came to him in a dream he abandoned the solitary lifestyle.

Asking for forgiveness, the younger Mack returned to the Brethren in 1748 and was reconciled and restored. He went on to became a great leader whose letters, daybook, devotional and doctrinal writings, and poetry reflect a desire for moderation, acceptance, and love. Along with the legendary Colonial printer Christopher Sauer II he was co-pastor of the Germantown congregation for the rest of his long life. (The two, in turn, each officiated at the other's wedding.)

No greater example of his temperament can be found than his words at the end of an essay in which he defends a particular order of worship for the love feast, but then reminds his readers that Jesus himself said we should be known as his disciples by our love for each other.

Asking for forgiveness, the younger Mack returned to the Brethren in 1748 and was reconciled and restored. He went on to became a great leader whose letters, daybook, devotional and doctrinal writings, and poetry reflect a desire for moderation, acceptance, and love.

Alexander Mack Jr.'s gravestone stands among those of other early Brethren in the Germantown cemetery in Philadelphia.

"GOTT
DER UNS HAT
AUS STAUB GEMACHT
UND WIEDERUM
ZUM STAUB GEBRACHT
WIRD ZEIGEN
SEINER WEISHEIT MACHT
WANN WIR NACH SEINEM
BILD ERWACHT."
ALEXANDER MACK
GEB 1712
GEST 1803
ALTER 91 JAHRE, 1 MONAT, 20 TAGE

Glenn R. Riegel

In this appendix to his father's *Rights and Ordinances,* Sander Mack lays out what he believes to be the only proper way to conduct the feetwashing portion of the love feast. He had such stature among the Brethren that he could, like Paul, have commanded certain behavior. However, even though he considers his interpretation the correct one, he emphasizes that he would rather concede to someone he considered wrong if that action would help preserve love than maintain his correct interpretation of scripture if it meant driving a wedge between believers.

He goes on to say that he would always give in to others because he "was especially concerned that the love and unity of the church not be lost," reminding his readers that Jesus said that believers would be recognized not by whether they got such details right but "rather that all 'shall know that you are my disciples, that you have love for one another.' " The passage continues: "Oh, how Satan could mock us if we were to quarrel with one another about the time when the feet should be washed, and love would be destroyed.... Therefore, dear brethren, let us watch and be careful, and above all preserve love, for thus one preserves light."

Mack's kindness and dedication to serve can be seen in his letters, preserved for the most part in the special collections at Juniata College and printed in Don Durnbaugh's sourcebook *The Brethren in Colonial America.* It was also evident in the way he cared for Johannes Lay in his home from December 15, 1758, until Lay's death on April 25 the following year. Mack injured his back so badly while trying to lift Ley that he had to hire outside help to assist him with his weaving business. By March Ley had contracted gangrene and "the stench was nearly unbearable." Yet Mack continued to provide care at great expense and inconvenience to himself.

Sander Mack and others saw to it that a love fund was collected for the maintenance of the poor in the congregation, and even those beyond the congrega-

> In every letter, every poem, every essay, it is clear that Mack is motivated by a **love for Jesus Christ and a desire to follow him**—in the company of other beloved believers.

tion. In his last recorded letter Mack, then age 91 and spiritual leader of the Brethren for more than half a century, wrote to the Germantown congregation—not to sum up his life or make some spiritual point, but to take them to task for not taking care of a widow who needed their aid.

Identifying himself as "an aged stranger and pilgrim on this earth," he admitted that the woman was very difficult and unstable, and though they could not readmit her to the flock, they could care for her. Initially the congregation had decided to give her a measure of flour every month. Then Mack, too weak to go to the council meeting, wrote, "I could not assume then that I would live to see New Year's Day, about four months hence. I did, however, have every right to assume that when the mortal shell of mine is buried, the New Testament is not buried with it. And it is there that the Lord speaks and says: 'It is more blessed to give than to receive!' "

He assumed they would add a pound of butter to the 'quarter' of flour they gave the widow every month, but he learned they took even the flour away. Quoting from an apocryphal book, Sirach 35:25, he said, "The poor man has nothing except a little bread; whoever deprives him of it, is a murderer." These last words of Mack foreshadow the strong Brethren emphasis on service to all that would characterize us in later centuries.

Sander Mack was no stranger to personal tragedy. Among the many family deaths he recorded in his day book, the most poignant was the death of his daughter Anna Marie, who on April 5, 1770, died at age 17 years, 5 months, and 7 days giving birth to a son. Mack suggested he could have been named Benoni, "a son of pain," in remembrance of the story of Benjamin in the book of Genesis, whose birth resulted in his mother Rachel's death. However, he chose to name him Jonas, "who was pulled from the stomach of the whale by the good hand of God as an example of conversion." Four months, five days, and 11 hours later Jonas followed his mother into death, a victim of cholera.

Without Sander Mack much important history would be lost. He wrote the first real history of the Brethren, published as a preface to his father's works. He also left behind an extensive list of Brethren who had died, a historical treasure trove. These, coupled with his published defense of Brethren doctrine and practice, provide the clearest window on the life of the church in both Colonial America and in the new nation.

In every letter, every poem, every essay, it is clear that Mack is motivated by a love for Jesus Christ and a desire to follow him—in the company of other beloved believers.

Small groups like ours can get so caught up in the search for perfection that we can split from each other time and again. The humorist Garrison Keillor, writing about the Sanctified Brethren among whom he grew up, speaks of their insistence on doctrinal purity: "Scholarly to the core and perfect literalists every one, they set to arguing over points that, to any outsider, would have seemed very minor indeed, but which to them were crucial to the Faith. . . ." He continues, "Once having tasted the pleasure of being Correct and defending True Doctrine, they kept right on and broke up at every opportunity until, by the time I came along, there were dozens of tiny Brethren groups, none of which were speaking to any of the others."

This could easily have been our story. Indeed, you can see this in action in the two splits recently experienced by our Grace Brethren cousins. The fact that splits have been the exception rather than the rule despite a contentious history of theological disagreements in our midst has to be, at least in part, a legacy of Sander Mack.

Beginning in 1772 Mack wrote a poem every year on his birthday. The poems consistently thank God for the years that have been granted and express trust in God and in the future. In addition, he wrote his own simple epitaph, which graces his tombstone. It reads:

God
Who us of dust did make
And again to dust will take
His wisdom like the sun shall break
When in his likeness we awake!

Alexander Mack Jr. died in 1803 at the age of 91 years, 1 month, and 20 days.

Conrad Beissel
and the Ephrata Cloister

by Christina Bucher

Elements of radical Pietist community survive today

The Ephrata Cloister, a religious community of radical Pietists, was founded in 1732 by a German immigrant named Conrad Beissel (1691-1768). For a short time, Beissel was a leader of the Brethren congregation at Conestoga, in Pennsylvania; however, he differed with the Brethren on several key points and left the Brethren in order to follow his own distinctive beliefs and practices.

Conrad Beissel. Beissel was born in 1691, in Eberbach am Neckar, in what is now Germany. Orphaned by age 8, Beissel became a baker. Beissel's family belonged to the Reformed tradition; however, as a youth, Beissel encountered radical Pietist groups and became convinced of the truth of their understanding of the Christian life. In his late 20s, Beissel emigrated to the New World, settling first in Germantown (near Philadelphia). There Beissel associated with Brethren, apprenticing himself to Peter Becker, a weaver and a leader in the Brethren movement.

Beissel soon moved west to Conestoga. In his early 30s, Beissel was baptized by Becker and became a leader of the Brethren at Conestoga. After only four years, however, Beissel withdrew from the congregation, and in 1732 he moved several miles north, settling along the banks of the Cocalico Creek.

Despite their austere lifestyle, the members of the Ephrata community produced beautiful examples of illuminated manuscripts, known as Fraktur, and engaged in singing hymns, many of them written by Beissel himself.

Courtesy of Brethren Historical Library and Archives

The Ephrata Cloister. Beissel was a charismatic leader, and several Brethren chose to follow him to Ephrata, where a religious community arose with Beissel as leader. The religious community at Ephrata, like the Brethren, observed believers baptism, love feast, and feetwashing, but they differed from Brethren in other significant ways. Believing that God had ordained the seventh day as a Sabbath, they observed Saturday as their primary day of worship.

Perhaps more provocatively, Beissel advocated celibacy as a Christian ideal, and the 18th-century community included both male and female celibate members. Despite Beissel's advocacy of celibacy, married individuals—known as householders—also lived as part of the Ephrata community. The monks, nuns, and householders of Ephrata followed a rigorous lifestyle devoted to prayer and worship. Believing that disciplined lives helped them stay close to God, they worked hard, slept and ate little, and enjoyed no luxuries.

Despite their austere lifestyle, the members of the Ephrata community produced beautiful examples of illuminated manuscripts, known as *Fraktur*, and engaged in singing hymns, many of them written by Beissel himself. Community members operated a paper mill, book bindery, oil mill, and tannery. They also ran a printing press for roughly half a century, printing hymnals, Bibles, the Mennonite *Martyrs Mirror*, and other works.

In the 1740s and 1750s, the Ephrata community swelled its ranks to more than 300 members. After Beissel's death in 1768, however, the community lost some of its momentum. The last celibate community member, a nun, died in 1813. The following year, Ephrata householders formed a group known as the

German Seventh-Day Baptist Church and continued weekly worship at Ephrata until the early 20th century.

Ephrata today. By the 20th century, the church had abandoned, along with the celibate life, many of Beissel's mystically influenced beliefs and practices; however, they continued to observe Saturday as their Sabbath. Time had taken its toll on the 18th-century buildings at Ephrata, and because church members did not have the funds to repair and maintain the historic buildings of the Cloister, they sold the property to the Commonwealth of Pennsylvania.

Although the German Seventh-Day Baptists at Ephrata suspended regular worship, two small congregations at Snow Hill (Franklin County, Pa.) and Salemville (Bedford County, Pa.) continue to hold weekly Sabbath services, and members travel twice a year to hold a love feast in the historic meeting house (known as the *Saal*) at the Ephrata Cloister. The Snow Hill and Salemville congregations were established in the 18th century as branch societies of the Ephrata community. Today, the Ephrata Cloister is a National Historic Landmark administered by the Pennsylvania Historical and Museum Commission. Many of the buildings erected in Beissel's time survive and offer visitors a glimpse into the beliefs and practices of an 18th-century radical Pietist community.

Courtesy of Brethren Historical Library and Archives

The Ephrata Cloister, founded by Conrad Beissel, has been maintained as a historical and educational site in Lancaster County, Pa.

A DUNKER GUIDE TO BRETHREN HISTORY

1808-1858
Moving onward & outward

THE WOLF

Medford D. Neher / Courtesy of Camp Mack

From 1808 to 1858: During the first half of the 19th century, Brethren crossed boundaries into new geographical territories and new ways of thinking about leadership. The western frontier provided challenges that led Brethren to take bold steps on issues of race and gender, but it also created theological tension between eastern and western Brethren.

Sarah Righter Major
Preaching with power
by Pamela K. Brubaker

Her 'uncommon' ministry stretched boundaries of Annual Meeting

Sarah Righter Major (1808-1884) was the first known Brethren woman to preach publicly. Her story is not only inspiring; it also offers insight into church polity and practice among 19th-century Brethren.

Sarah was born to John and Elisabeth (Stern) Righter on August 29, 1808, in Germantown, Pa. She was not yet a member of the church when she heard Harriet Livermore preach in August of 1826. Livermore was a writer, teacher, and traveling evangelist who called herself "The Pilgrim Stranger."

Livermore had been invited to preach by Peter Keyser Jr., pastor of the Germantown and Philadelphia congregations. Sarah's son later wrote, "Here it was that my mother heard The Pilgrim Stranger and as the first fruits of her labors in Philadelphia was the conversion of my mother whom Harriet Livermore ever afterwards called 'my daughter' as Paul called Timothy his son, and was not lacking in parental solicitude for her welfare."

Sarah was baptized on November 12, 1826, according to the records of the Philadelphia congregation. Shortly thereafter she felt a call to preach, but know-

A committee of elders was sent to silence her, but after hearing her preach could not do so. Elder James H. Tracy explained, **"I could not give my voice to silence someone who could outpreach me."**

Courtesy of Brethren Historical Library and Archives

ing the views of the Brethren was fearful of doing so. Sensing her distress, her father asked what was troubling her. After she told him of her call, they went together to consult Brother Peter Keyser. He helped her overcome her fears and to begin speaking. Elder Israel Poulson invited her to speak at the Amwell, N.J., congregation. Her preaching seemed inspired, and several other congregations invited her to come and hold evangelistic meetings. Abraham Harley Cassel, one of her converts and a noted Brethren antiquarian, wrote, "I have heard many sermons, but none ever surpassed hers."

Sarah's preaching came to the attention of the 1834 Annual Meeting, where it was strongly disapproved on grounds of scripture and the ancient order of the church. In addition, it was charged that "Such sister being in danger, not only exposing her own state of grace to temptation, but also causing temptations, discord, and disputes among other members."

A committee of elders was sent to silence her, but after hearing her preach could not do so. Elder James H. Tracy explained, "I could not give my voice to silence someone who could outpreach me." Sarah defended herself in a letter written in 1835 to printer Jacob Sala: "I conceive it would be very inconsistent in an apostle [Paul], who had laid his hands on men and women, and pray'd over them that they might receive the Holy Ghost, to quench the gift of the spirit of God because it was given to a woman—in answer to prayer—when at that time it may not be given in such measure to more mature Christians."

Sarah's life changed again when she married Thomas Major (1811-1888) on March 10, 1842. Major was a carpenter who had boarded in the Righter home. In 1841 he and John Righter (Sarah's father) were elected to the Brethren ministry. In the spring of 1843, Sarah and Thomas moved to Ohio, first to Scioto County and then to Highland County (southeast of Dayton). There they farmed and supplemented their income with Thomas' carpentry work. Five children were born to them, although the first was stillborn and the second died at three months of age.

Courtesy of Brethren Historical Library and Archives

Sarah and Thomas both seem to have been **guided by their own strong sense of calling,** carrying out a ministry not always authorized by US law or Annual Meeting.

Thomas and Sarah continued to preach in Ohio, without remuneration. Family records indicate, "Each Sunday they held from one to three services, often traveling a distance of ten to fifteen miles over poor roads to meet those eagerly gathered to listen to them. Their joint efforts resulted in the building of a church at what was then called New Lexington." According to various people who heard Sarah preach, she usually sat with the congregation until invited by her husband to come up to preach. If the congregation had asked that Sarah not preach, she would often lead in prayer. The Majors also preached in homes, infirmaries, and prisons.

In Ohio, Sarah and Thomas helped resettle freed slaves from the South. Their involvement with Samuel Weir, the first African-American Brethren minister, was recounted by Elder Landon West in a pamphlet in 1897. Brother B.F. Moomaw of Virginia brought Sam, who was at the time illiterate, to Ohio, where he told him, "Sam, you are now a free man and on free soil, where you can enjoy your freedom as all other free men." They traveled to the home of the Majors, where Sarah received and cared for them since Thomas was away from home. Sarah and Thomas became friends and supporters of Samuel, who learned to read and write and study the Bible. Eventually he began to preach and was then elected to the ministry. In October 1865, the Majors were the first "white" Brethren to participate in an integrated love feast. In addition to Samuel, the recently baptized Harvey and Martha Carter participated. In 1872, Brother Carter was also called to the Brethren ministry.

Only recently have we learned from family records made available to Nancy Kettering Frye (*Uncommon Woman: The Life and Times of Sarah Righter Major*, Brethren Press, 1997) that Thomas and Sarah "were very active in the movement for the abolition of slavery[,] their farm was a stop on the 'Underground

Rail[way],' which conveyed slaves to Canada for freedom." As early as 1782, Annual Meeting had opposed slavery: "Concerning the unchristian negro slave trade, it has been unanimously considered, that it cannot be permitted in any wise by the church, that a member should or could purchase negroes, or keep them as slaves. . . ." As family records indicate, the Majors went further, opposing the slave trade itself and breaking the Fugitive Slave Act of 1850, which required citizens to assist in the capture of fugitive slaves.

Sarah and Thomas both seem to have been guided by their own strong sense of calling, carrying out a ministry not always authorized by US law or Annual Meeting. Its stern 1834 decision against women preaching was slightly revised in 1858, when women were granted permission to pray and prophesy but not to preach.

However, in 1878 Sarah preached to overflow crowds at the Annual Meeting in North Manchester, Ind. Some of her contemporaries, such as Brother J.H. Warstler of Indiana, described her as "the picture of meekness and humility, completely subject to the will of her husband." Perhaps, but her marriage may have been based on the view of mutuality she expressed in her 1835 letter: "I believe man to have been first in creation, but I also believe woman was made to be an help meet for or equal to him, having a soul and body, capable of helping him, in his natural, and spiritual world. . . ."

Sarah and Thomas worked as a team, sensitive to the feelings of those who did not share their understanding of their call, but forging ahead nevertheless. And the church never prohibited them, once they experienced the inspiration and power of their ministry. We can learn much from this approach to controversy about who is permitted to preach and minister in our midst.

The Wolfes
Leading the way west
by James Benedict

**Three generations of family gave key leadership
to frontier church**

In the great western migration that defined the late 18th and the 19th century in North America, Brethren were largely non-participants. To this day, the vast majority of Brethren in the United States live within a few hundred miles of the Atlantic Ocean. But a few brave Dunker families did go west, and among them none had a bigger impact on the life of the church than the Wolfe family. In the course of three generations, they carried the Brethren message from Lancaster County, Pa., to the Pacific slope of California.

It just so happens that in each generation of the Wolfe family, the boldest pioneer was named George. It began with George Sr., born in Lancaster County in

Medford D. Neher / Courtesy of Camp Mack

1750. Most likely ordained to the ministry there, at age 37 he moved his young family to Fayette County, Pa. It isn't far by modern standards, but in those days the distance was significant. Lancaster County was well established; Fayette County was essentially frontier wilderness.

But evidently it was not wilderness enough for the Wolfe family. After 13 years there, George Sr. and his

Courtesy of Brethren Historical Library and Archives

sons built a flatboat and migrated down the Ohio River to Logan County in far western Kentucky. Other Brethren accompanied them, and George Sr. continued the work of ministry, including preaching forays into what is now southeast Missouri and southern Illinois. In fact, it was while on a preaching tour in Illinois that George Sr. died suddenly in 1809.

By that time, George Jr. (pictured) had married and left Kentucky with a brother Jacob and brother-in-law Abraham Hunsacker, heading farther west. Not far from the settlement of Cape Girardeau, they encountered excellent hunting near present-day Jonesboro, Ill. With only guns, ammunition, corn, and a few tools, they set to work building shelter. They then returned to Kentucky and brought their families to the area, becoming the first non-Native American residents of what became Union County.

Though the son of a minister, married, and nearly 30 years old, George Jr. had not yet been baptized. Apparently religion was not a major concern. All that changed, however, when the earth shook. In the winter of 1811-1812, the infamous New Madrid earthquake sent several shocks through the area, the biggest of all on Feb. 7, 1812. Estimated at 8.0 or higher on the Richter scale, it created new lakes, changed the course of the Mississippi, and even cracked sidewalks as far away as Washington, D.C. In addition to dramatic changes in the geography of the area and a number of deaths, the quake also caused a religious revival. One eyewitness reported, "A lot of people thinks (sic) that the devil has come here. Some thinks (sic) that this is the beginning of the world coming to a (sic) end."

The Methodists were first to capitalize on the new religious fervor among the settlers. A circuit rider formed a class in the community and made George the class leader. It wasn't long, though, before the Brethren heritage of most members of the class led them to seek guidance from Brethren in Kentucky. One of their number was sent to fetch John Hendricks, a Brethren minister. In what must have seemed to them a clear sign of God's approval of their decision, it turned out that Hendricks was already on his way to visit them. The messenger they had sent met Hendricks halfway. Shortly thereafter, 14 people—including George Jr. and his wife Ann—were baptized.

A few months later, Hendricks returned to establish a formal congregation and to oversee the election of George Jr. to the ministry. Initially reluctant to accept the call, Wolfe proved to be an able leader. He was a large man, more than 6 feet tall and weighing 275 pounds, but he was known as much for his intelligence, good sense, and kindness as for his size. He established a strong congregation in Union County, and traveled to encourage Brethren elsewhere in the region.

In 1831, George Jr. and his family were part of a migration of 20 or so Brethren families northward from Union County to Adams County. There he helped organize the Mill Creek congregation. A successful farmer, he also found time to continue his preaching and his visits with other congregations of what came to be called the Far Western Brethren.

The leadership of George Wolfe Jr. among the Far Western Brethren proved critical. Time, distance, and other factors had led to the development of significant differences between the Far Western Brethren and the Brethren back in the East. Two differences were especially problematic. First, the Far Western Brethren believed in universal restoration. Universal restoration is the belief that all people will ultimately enjoy salvation, although some only after a period of punishment. This had been a minority view among Brethren, possibly from the earliest days in Germany, but in the first half of the 19th century it was frowned upon by the majority of Brethren in Pennsylvania, Maryland, and Virginia.

The second difference between Brethren in the East and Far Western Brethren was even more controversial. It regarded the proper way to practice love feast. Far Western Brethren practiced the "single mode," in which each participant would wash and dry the feet of one other person. Brethren in the East, on the other hand, practiced the "double mode," in which a pair of members would rise from the table, one taking the basin and the other the towel, and they would proceed to wash and dry the feet of several others.

Far Western Brethren resisted, and **without the wise and patient leadership of George Wolfe Jr. there could have been a permanent split.** Wolfe and a few other of the Far Western Brethren did not give up. They met and crafted a compromise.

As new waves of Brethren began to come west, the difference became problematic. Newer settlers complained that the "single mode" was contrary to tradition. Older settlers, including Wolfe and others, insisted that the "single mode" was actually the most ancient and proper way. Eventually the disagreement over feetwashing and questions about universal restoration made it all the way to Annual Meeting. Brethren in the East being so much more numerous, the outcome was predictable. Annual Meeting declared that the Far Western Brethren were in error and must change.

Far Western Brethren resisted, and without the wise and patient leadership of George Wolfe Jr. there could have been a permanent split. Wolfe and a few other of the Far Western Brethren did not give up. They met and crafted a compromise. Although this compromise was also initially rejected by Annual Meeting, five years later its essentials were included in an Annual Meeting decision that preserved the unity of the church.

George Wolfe Jr. remained an effective and respected leader in Illinois until his death in 1865. By then his nephew and namesake, George Wolfe III, had completed the family journey across the continent. Born in 1809 in Union County, Ill., George III was baptized in 1833. Ten years later he was ordained by two elders: his uncle and Charles Doughterly. After a few years of service in Iowa and Illinois, the urge to head west struck the third generation as forcefully as it had the first two. George III headed for California, where he organized the first congregation and presided over the Brethren for 35 years.

Courage and a sense of adventure never seemed in short supply in the Wolfe family. Three generations of Georges led the way as Brethren headed west. But the most important contribution from the Wolfe family was the strong but gentle leadership of George Jr., who helped a church dangerously close to schism reach a compromise—proving pioneers can also be peacemakers.

Samuel Weir
African-American preacher and elder

by Anna M. Speicher

Ministry gifts prompted outreach to blacks in Ohio

amuel Weir was born a slave, in Bath County, Va., April 15, 1812. So begins an 1896 sketch of the life of a remarkable man. Weir's life story is a testimony to gracious perseverance in the face of many obstacles.

When Samuel Weir was 12 years old, he experienced one of the heartbreaks of slavery: For the price of $280 he was sold away from the rest of his family, enslaved to a Virginia landowner. Weir was fortunate only in that his buyer, Andrew McClure, treated him relatively well. McClure was a farmer who labored in the fields alongside Weir. Young Samuel retained a measure of autonomy in keeping the surname of his father, James Weir, rather than adopting the name of his owners as many slaves did.

Weir's enslavement continued for 19 years. It ended because of tragedy in the McClure family. When the son of the family was killed in a horseback riding accident, the McClures turned to religion and soon petitioned to become members of the local Brethren congregation. For the Dunkers, though, the existence of a slave in the household was grounds for denial of membership. Unlike most other American faith groups at that time, the Brethren had been officially antislavery since the Annual Meeting of 1782. The minutes of that meeting recorded that "it can not be permitted in any wise by the church, that a member should or could purchase negroes, or keep them as slaves."

The McClures' religious conversion was genuine enough that they were willing to give up their free labor in order to join the church. And their adoption of Brethren

Kermon Thomasson /Brethren Historical Library and Archives

views was in more than name only: McClure refused an offer of $1,500 for the now 31-year-old Weir, claiming he was now "opposed to the sale of humanity." McClure freed Weir, and the McClures were baptized Brethren in February 1843.

Weir continued to work for McClure as a field hand for the next eight months. Like his former owners, Weir was also attracted to the Brethren way of belief and life. When the local Methodist minister told him they had been "fishing for [the McClures] this long time, but we didn't catch them," Weir replied, "Brother, you didn't fish in deep enough water." Weir also was baptized into the church in May 1843, becoming the first black member in that part of Virginia. Unfortunately, being antislavery in principle did not make Dunkers egalitarian in practice. Weir was received into Brethren fellowship with the right hand of fellowship, but the congregation declined to welcome him with the usual kiss of charity.

As a freedman, it was not possible for Weir to remain in Virginia. By law, any emancipated slave was required to leave the state within one year or be subject to re-enslavement. Fortunately, a white brother, B.F. Moomaw, was planning to travel to the free state of Ohio and offered to take Weir along with him. This was critical, as free blacks traveling alone through slave states risked capture by unscrupulous whites.

> He began to preach at these meetings and was eventually invited to address an all-white Brethren audience. The Paint Creek congregation in southern Ohio called him to the ministry in 1849 and charged him to **travel and preach to blacks wherever he could.**

In Paint Creek, Ohio, William Bryant offered to house Weir. Weir lived with the Bryants and worked there as a farm hand for the next two years. The Bryants offered not only lodging but the services of their 10-year-old granddaughter as a reading and writing teacher. The different light of that time shows, however, in Weir's recounting—without malice—that Katy would sometimes lose patience with his progress and tell him that he was "nothing but a black Negro, and that she could do nothing more for me." Weir said that he would approach her the following evening saying, "Now, Miss Katy, please try me again; I will do better this time."

Weir moved to Highland County, Ohio, and continued his studies, although he said, "When I found that I could read the Bible I was satisfied, and I gave up all other books but that." As in Virginia, the local Brethren congregations were willing to admit African Americans to membership but did not welcome them to attend worship services, so Weir attended meetings at black Baptist churches. He began to preach at these meetings and was eventually invited to address an all-white Brethren audience. The Paint Creek congregation in southern Ohio called him to the ministry in 1849 and charged him to travel and preach to blacks wherever he could.

Weir traveled and preached for 16 years before he succeeded in winning anyone to baptism. Harvey and Martha Carter were baptized in August 1856, and they and Weir formed the Franklin Colored Church, celebrating their first love feast in October (which was attended by Thomas and Sarah Righter Major). In 1872 Weir was authorized to baptize and conduct weddings, and in 1881 he was further ordained as an elder, with the responsibility for overseeing "all the colored members in the Scioto Valley." After nearly four decades of ministry, Samuel Weir died in March 1884, requesting that his home and property be transferred to the "colored brethren" of the Scioto Valley for a meeting place.

Weir's life is a lesson for us today in humility and persistence. It is also a reminder that we should examine ourselves for lingering prejudices that we may harbor in spite of our caring hearts and good intentions.

1808-1858

Westward ho, Brethren!
Groups gradually moved across nation

by Jane Davis

After receiving a Spanish land grant in 1796, Pennsylvanian Daniel Clingingsmith moved his family by boat down the Ohio River and then up the Mississippi to a new settlement in southeastern Missouri called Cape Girardeau. Brethren members of George Frederick Bollinger's wagon caravan from North Carolina (1800) and Brethren from western Kentucky soon added to the settlement along the Whitewater River near Cape Girardeau.

By 1806, Kentucky elder George Wolfe Sr., minister to the scattered Brethren along the Ohio and Mississippi rivers, had moved to Cape Girardeau. Whether he traveled north of St. Louis to visit the Hostetter Brethren near Saint Charles is unknown. We do know Wolfe became ill in traveling from Kaskaskia, Ill., to Ste. Genevieve, Mo. His verbal will is recorded there, as are the names of those verifying his identity at his death on August 8, 1808. The Hostetter family began arriving in northern Missouri from Kentucky after receiving a land grant about 1797. Brethren elder Francis Hostetter (1739-1806) was one of the earliest Protestant ministers in northeastern Missouri, preaching in German to English-speaking listeners.

The majority of Missouri and early Illinois Brethren were part of the movement out of North Carolina following the split over universalism and love feast practices. Southern Brethren followed the opening of lands westward into states bordering the Ohio River. Responses to frontier living and religious movements led Brethren to resolve issues of baptism, love feast, slave-holding, oath-taking, and military stance in different ways. While most of the southern Indiana and eastern

Southern Brethren **followed the opening of lands westward** into states bordering the Ohio River. Responses to frontier living and religious movements led Brethren to resolve issues of baptism, love feast, slave-holding, oath-taking, and military stance in different ways.

Kentucky Brethren were lost to the German Baptist Brethren, many western Kentucky Brethren moved into southern Illinois and Missouri, establishing the Clear Creek congregation (Ill.) and the Whitewater congregation (Mo.) in 1812. Under the leadership of elders George Wolfe and James Hendricks (from Kentucky), these churches flourished.

By 1827 they began moving north to near Quincy in Adams County, Ill., organizing the Mill Creek congregation in 1831 with George Wolfe as elder. Members from this congregation soon established new church organizations in Illinois; Libertyville, Iowa (1844); and northern Missouri. A caravan of Mill Creek members arrived in Oregon in 1852, a second group in California in 1856.

By 1858 Brethren were scattered across Missouri. They represented mainline Brethren from Pennsylvania, Virginia, Ohio, Indiana, and Illinois, with concentrations in west-central, southwestern, and northwestern Missouri. Missouri Brethren lived peaceably beside their slave-holding neighbors until the Civil War erupted around them early in 1861. Too scattered and isolated yet to organize as a district, Missouri Brethren maintained some contact with Brethren in Iowa, Illinois, and later Kansas.

When the Kansas Territory opened for settlement in 1854, Brethren were among the first to arrive. Early church organizations were near Emporia (1856) and south of Lawrence in Douglas County (1858). Situated along the Oregon and Santa Fe trails, the Douglas County Brethren hosted many arriving settlers. Early visitors included John Brown and James Lane, soon to figure prominently in the border warfare between Kansas and Missouri (1854-1861). Brethren also checked out the gold fields of California in 1849 and those of Denver, Colo., in 1858.

Israel Poulson Sr.
Breaking the mold
by Frank Ramirez

**His famous 'three visions' included
scenes of Last Judgment**

There's a tendency to think of the old Brethren elders as "one size fits all," but even when they sought uniformity in faith and practice, they still tended to be unique figures. Certainly Israel Poulson Sr. followed the pattern of not following a pattern.

First, he was half Native American in a largely German church. Second, he played the fiddle when Brethren sang *a capella*. And finally, he was a dreamer, and he told people about his dreams.

Israel Poulson (1770-1856) was abandoned by his parents when he was seven years old. He was raised by Brethren near Centerville, N.J. When he first married he was unable to read or write, but his first wife taught him those skills. When she died he married her sister. All his children were born through her. He married a third time after her death.

Poulson was much beloved by the children and trusted by his neighbors. Once a man called a "false prophet" announced that the world was about to come to an end and asked what people intended to do. One individual who was developmentally disabled had a quick answer: "I would hold on to Uncle Israel's coat-tail."

Prior to the 20th century, Brethren pastors earned their living as farmers and in various trades, usually cobbling together more than one position. Israel Poulson was a farmer, like most Brethren. He was also literally a fence mender. He built fences. He built homes. A stonemason, he built walls.

But he was also active in civic affairs. He was made assessor for Amwell Township in New Jersey when he announced that $300 was too large a sum for the job, and that he would do it for $100. He was also the tax collector. To facilitate collections, his notice in the November 2, 1829, number of the *Hunterton*

> First, he was half Native American in a largely German church. Second, he played the fiddle when Brethren sang *a capella*. And finally, **he was a dreamer, and he told people about his dreams.**

County Gazette encouraged early payment and included a little poem (see p. 64).

Poulson was singular in his appearance. It was remembered that, "He was not particular in the form of his dress, yet intended to conform to the order of the Brotherhood," according to biographical reports, and that he was known for two props, a cane and a pipe, which accompanied him as he cut across fields to make visits. More important, he was part of the transition among the Brethren from a German-speaking to an English-speaking church. The popular preacher and storyteller spoke primarily in English.

A bit of an outsider himself, Poulson encouraged the ministry of Sarah Righter Major by becoming the first to invite her to preach outside Philadelphia, her home church. Though based in New Jersey, he was recognized as an elder at the 1848 Annual Meeting and was widely respected. Perhaps the one blot on his record, in the mind of his contemporaries, was his son, Israel Poulson Jr., whose abrasive form of leadership led to a schism in the Amwell congregation after the elder Poulson's death.

His famous three visions were recorded in the reminiscences of 19th-century Brethren historian and book collector Abraham Harley Cassel, published in *The History of the Church of the Brethren in Eastern Pennsylvania in 1915.*

The first two, "The Laborers by the Way" and "The Old Fiddle," concerned the importance of the attitude we bring to our Christian work and the danger of preaching the same old sermon over and over. But the one he called "The Loaf of Bread" was the most compelling.

Told in dramatic fashion, the dream found him "in an immense concourse of people" who were milling forward toward who-knew-what goal? Far in the distance he could see a giant set of scales. To his alarm he realized he had found himself at the Last Judgment. Many of those who stepped on the scales were too light to hold them down. It was no better when his turn came. His heart was failing him as he heard the judge pronounce, "Weighed and found wanting." But before words of condemnation could be spoken, a boy ran forward through the crowd and tossed him a loaf of bread. Down came the scale. The judge pronounced, "Accepted." Only then did he recognize the loaf as one he had once given to a widow.

The vision is a reminder that Brethren lived with the tension found in New Testament books such as Romans and Galatians on one hand, versus Matthew 25 and the letter of James on the other. Brethren believed in salvation by faith, but believed that faith without works was dead. The two were different sides of the same coin. Self-educated Brethren pastors did not spend their time in church offices. Their daily lives in their professions and their ministries took place in the real world. Rather than resolve the tension, they lived the gospel.

Poulson's ministry is a reminder that there was never a period when the Brethren experience was crystallized in a perfect stasis. The life of a highly respected half Native American preacher who spoke English and encouraged women in ministry is a reminder that the Brethren experience has always been in flux.

POETIC (TAX) LICENSE

Tax collector Israel Poulson Sr. encouraged Amwell, N.J., residents to avoid late fees with the following bit of doggerel:

There's one thing more you may remember:
Unless 'tis paid by the twentieth December,
Of course there will be two cents cost,
Which will be so much to you lost.
And if not paid in five days more,
An additional sum of thirty-four.
The law is plain, you all may see;
Then I would have you not blame me;
If I return you to the Squire
'Twill be just what the laws require."

(from The Brethren Encyclopedia, *p. 1049)*

1858-1908
Together and apart

Albert Winkler / Courtesy of BHLA

From 1858 to 1908: The last half of the 19th century was an era when Brethren stayed together through the Civil War before experiencing schisms of their own. Although respected leaders such as John Kline and James Quinter sought to keep the church together, larger societal issues led to a denominational three-way split.

John Kline
A beloved man of God
by Paul Roth

Virginian led Brethren through turbulent Civil War years

The old pine floorboards in John Kline's house are bare now. The footsteps of this beloved Brethren elder have not been heard on them for 144 years. Yet memories still linger about this 19th-century missionary, herbal doctor, Annual Meeting moderator, farmer, and friend.

John Kline was born June 17, 1797, in Dauphin County, Pa., the second child and first son of John Sr. and Mary Hershey Kline. His grandparents George Jr. and Elizabeth Altaffer Klein were among the early settlers to the Shenandoah Valley of Virginia in the 1780s, buying several acres on the west side of Linville Creek near the trading post known as Broadway. John Kline Sr. moved his family to take over George Klein Jr.'s farm in 1811, with John Jr. driving the horse-drawn wagon.

Writing in "Elder John Kline: A life of pacifism ended in martyrdom" (*Virginia Cavalcade*, Autumn 1964), Klaus G. Wust

Medford D. Neher / Courtesy of Camp Mack

> I am now on my way back to Virginia, not knowing the things that shall befall me there. None of these things move me; neither count I my life dear unto myself, **so that I may finish my course with joy.**

comments, "He went to school very seldom while he lived in Pennsylvania, but his parents, the preacher, and family friends instructed the boy in the essentials of learning. He was trained to read and write both in German and in English and acquired whatever arithmetic a farm boy ought to know. John Kline had a great penchant for reading; unlike most Valley Germans of that period, he not only read religious works, but eagerly consumed everything he found in print."

John Kline Jr. would marry Anna Wampler, daughter of early Brethren settlers John and Magdalene Garber Wampler, on March 18, 1818. Their home was built in 1822 on land given to him by his father. Its interior construction allowed for movable walls to be hung from the ceiling for the eight to 12 families who would come for worship. The meetinghouse worship rotated between the 1794 Yount house (now Tunker House) across the road and his younger brother Samuel Kline's 1830 house on their grandfather's farm on the west side of Linville Creek.

John and Anna Kline had only one child, a daughter, who died shortly after birth on March 15, 1819, and is buried in the family cemetery near his grandparents' graves on the original farm. With no other children, Kline would nurture a love for youth throughout his life, paying indentures for young boys to learn the farming trade and creating a school (The Cedar Grove Academy) on his farm for their education. On frequent visits to the homes of members or on missionary trips, Kline would find an opportunity to speak to youth about a life of devotion and discipleship to Jesus Christ and service to others.

In 1825, Kline gave part of his farmland to the Linville Creek congregation "for religious purposes." The congregation recognized his zeal for ministry and elected him deacon in 1827. He was chosen to be a minister in 1830. On February 8, 1835, he preached his first sermon. He then embarked on his first missionary journey with Elder Daniel Miller to neighboring counties, a relationship that continued frequently with Elder Miller preaching in German and Kline following in English. Kline's creative use of real-life experiences in his sermons made him a welcomed guest in every home. Many congregations in Virginia, West Virginia, Tennessee, Kentucky, and Ohio began from his missionary trips.

These preaching journeys impressed upon Kline the poverty of the mountain folk. Frequently he shared wheat or produce from his farm, even a few dollars from his pocket, to relieve their struggle. He would talk to them about Jesus Christ, and out of compassion for their ignorance of the outside world he offered practical advice for daily living.

It may have been such visits to rural, mountainous regions that led Kline to explore herbal medicine. His January 1, 1836, diary entry records his interest in the work of Dr. Samuel Thompson of Vermont, who "is introducing a new system of medical practice which I believe to be more in accordance with the laws of life and health than any I know of. His maxim, applied to disease, is: 'Remove the cause, and the effect will cease.' "

Kline would use his missionary travels to coincide when particular roots and herbs could be harvested. Returning home, he would dry the herbs and create potions for ingestion or application to a wound to naturally restore the individual to health. His practice brought reasonably better results than harsher traditional medical practice, so he was called upon frequently to visit neighbors. During the Civil War, Kline was enlisted by nearby Union and Confederate camps to treat the wounded.

His faithful ministry resulted in ordination as an elder on April 13, 1848. He frequently helped in discernment of Annual Meeting decisions, especially clarifying the Brethren position on slavery in 1853. The encroachment of a War Between the States prompted Elder Kline to pen this entry to his diary on January 1, 1861: "The year opens with dark and lowering clouds in our national horizon. I feel a deep interest in the peace and prosperity of our country; but in my view both are sorely threatened now. . . . Secession means war; and war means tears and ashes and blood. It means bonds and imprisonments, and perhaps even death to many in our beloved Brotherhood, who, I have the confidence to believe, will die, rather than disobey God by taking up arms." Later that spring he would be elected as Annual Meeting moderator, a post he served until the spring of 1864.

His passion for non-resistance led Kline to write to Governor Letcher of Virginia and legislators John Hopkins, John C. Woodson, and Charles Lewis, explaining the faith and disciplines of the Brethren, as well as the Mennonites. He feared a draft would force these peace people to violate or compromise their faith, so he appealed for an exemption from military service. His efforts suc-

DID YOU KNOW?
The John Kline Memorial Riders follow trails frequented by the historic preacher to share history, fellowship, and worship with churches in Virginia, West Virginia, and Pennsylvania. Organized and led by Emmert Bittinger, the riders have been hosted by more than 30 churches.

ceeded in the Exemption Act passed March 29, 1862, for anyone who is "bona fide prevented from bearing arms, by the tenets of the church to which said applicant belongs," including a payment of $500 plus 2 percent of the assessed value of the applicant's taxable property. Kline helped to raise these exemption fees, paying many from his own resources. Just after this, Kline would be imprisoned with other Brethren and Mennonite leaders in the jury room of the Rockingham County courthouse on April 5, 1862, because of their opposition to the war.

Kline's diary editor, Benjamin Funk, makes this comment at the beginning of 1862: "At this time medicines were scarce and [also] physicians in the army. As a consequence of this the demands for Brother Kline's professional services as a physician were largely increased. The Diary for this year shows an almost incredible amount of labor performed by him in this line. . . . He had no day of rest. In connection with all this labor and responsibility, the Brotherhood looked to him for counsel and comfort on every hand. At the same time, he wrote many letters, not only to distant Brethren, but to men in civil and military place and power."

Kline's freedom of movement during the Civil War and frequent travels across battle lines raised several threats on his life. He would say in closing remarks on May 19, 1864, to Brethren gathered at the Annual Meeting in Hagerstown, Ind., "Possibly you may never see my face or hear my voice again. I am now on my way back to Virginia, not knowing the things that shall befall me there. It may be that bonds and afflictions abide me. But I feel that I have done nothing worthy of bonds or of death; and none of these things move me; neither count I my life dear unto myself, so that I may finish my course with joy, and the ministry which I have received of the Lord Jesus, to testify the Gospel of the grace of God."

After repairing a clock at a church member's house four miles west of his home, Elder John Kline was killed June 15, 1864, by a few local military irregulars unsympathetic to his cause.

Roger Sappington summarized the contributions of John Kline to the church in his epilogue of *Courageous Prophet*: "He was a good steward, who used his property and his life well. He was a good pastor, attending to the spiritual needs of others, especially to the young and the aged. He was a missionary with a passion for the unchurched. He was a diligent physician and progressive scientist. He was an articulate and ardent defender of the Brethren faith. He was a social activist for eliminating slavery, opposing war, and working to settle disputes with reason and respect. He was a courageous prophet, speaking frequently and widely to social concerns. And finally, John Kline was a dedicated Christian who used all of the personal strength and the physical prosperity which God had given him for the glory of God and his neighbor's good. When the time came for him to give his life rather than turn his back on his God, he gave his life. No man could ask more than this of a man of God!"

James Quinter
Gentle, persistent progressive

by J. Douglas Archer

**Respected Brethren leader championed
periodicals, higher education**

J ames Quinter was born in 1816 in Philadelphia. At that time the
Brethren supported no schools or colleges and had no regular publications
or publishing houses. By the time of Brother Quinter's death in 1888 this had
changed dramatically—thanks in large part to his efforts.

Almost all of what we know of his early life can be traced to the *Life and
Sermons of Elder James Quinter* (1891), by his daughter Mary. Raised in poverty
near Phoenixville, Pa., and breadwinner for his mother and sister from the death
of his father when he was 13, Quinter lacked all but the most basic formal schooling. However, what his family lacked in material resources was more than equaled
by a passion for education. By 1833, at age 17, Quinter managed to qualify for a
teaching position, and he appears to have been one of the first Dunkers to be
employed as an teacher. While he held several jobs over the years, education—
especially higher education—remained an enduring commitment.

His other unswerving commitment was to the church. He was called to ministry and ordained in 1838 by the Coventry congregation. At age 22 this was
rather unusual and a testimonial to his abilities, since most pastors were expected to have established themselves in their communities by occupation and marriage before being called. For the next several years he served a series of congregations and their surrounding communities, becoming known as the traveling
boy preacher or simply the English preacher. He was ordained an elder in the
Mill Creek (Mahoning) congregation in 1856.

Courtesy of Brethren Historical Library and Archives

In 1851, when Henry Kurtz began publishing the *Gospel Visitor*, Quinter contributed to its first issues under the name Clement. Before long he was its associate editor, adding a new theme to his life and ministry. Over the next several decades he published a series of periodicals, first in partnership with Kurtz (eventually buying his interest in the *Gospel Visitor*), then with Henry Holsinger, and finally with the Brumbaugh brothers. This string of periodicals (the *Gospel Visitor*, the *Christian Family Companion*, the *Pilgrim*, the *Primitive Christian*, and *Brethren at Work*) culminated in the *Gospel Messenger* in 1883.

Quinter was also responsible for another publishing milestone. While several hymnals had been published by Brethren in America, starting with *Das kleine Davidische Psalterspiel* (1744), Quinter was charged by Annual Conference with preparing the first authorized Brethren hymnal. Titled the *Brethren's Hymn Book* or *A Collection of Psalms, Hymns and Spiritual Songs,* it appeared in 1867. It contained 818 hymns in a pocket edition (text only, no tunes) and was well and widely received, being reprinted several times.

If Kurtz was the groundbreaking pioneer of Brethren publishing, then Quinter was the homesteader who settled in for the long haul, cleared the land, and raised the first sustained crops. This is a pattern also to be found Quinter's support for education.

Not surprising given his early years, Quinter was a strong and persistent advocate of higher education. In 1861 he helped found the New Vienna Academy in southern Ohio. Unfortunately, it suffered the same fate as many such Brethren ventures, failing in 1864. Undeterred, he was an early and strong supporter of the Brethren Normal School in Huntingdon, Pa., started in 1876, that later became Juniata College, the oldest surviving Brethren institution of higher learning. When its founder and principal, Jacob Zuck, died in 1879, Quinter was named president.

As with his efforts as a writer and publisher, playing homesteader to Kurtz's pioneer, he once again picked up work started by someone else and carried it forward with energy, creativity, and persistence. He served as Juniata's president for nine years until his death in 1888.

During the middle decades of the 1800s, Quinter developed quite a reputation as a defender of Brethren life and teachings in print and in person. In addition to his periodicals, Quinter published several pamphlets. Most notable of the pamphlets was *Trine Immersion,* published in 1886, the culmination of a life-long fascination with the subject of baptism.

By all accounts a very effective speaker, Quinter was frequently called upon to defend his church in public debate. However, he was careful to treat his opponents fairly, an approach that was not necessarily common in the public disputations of that era. Henry R. Holsinger, in his *History of the Tunkers and the Brethren Church* (1901), recounted one of those debates.

Courtesy of BHLA

Henry R. Holsinger

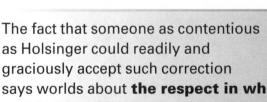

The fact that someone as contentious as Holsinger could readily and graciously accept such correction says worlds about **the respect in which Quinter was held by Holsinger and by the Church at large during this turbulent time.**

DID YOU KNOW?

The town of Quinter, founded by Brethren in 1885, was named for James Quinter. It is in northwestern Kansas and home to Quinter Church of the Brethren. Juniata College has a Quinter House on its campus, which houses the offices for many of the English faculty. Camp Alexander Mack in Milford, Ind., features the large Quinter-Miller Auditorium. And Quinter Memorial Hospital in Bulsar, India, was named for Quinter's daughter, Mary, a missionary to India.

He accompanied Quinter to the event and opened the proceedings with prayer. Holsinger "asked for a special blessing for Brother Quinter, that he might be enabled to successfully defend the truth." Then, to be "impartial," Holsinger prayed "that the Lord would give him [the other fellow] light to see his error and accept the better way." Quinter's opponent got the point—and was not pleased.

On the way home after the event Holsinger reports that Quinter gently called him to task for his partisan prayers, saying that he should "be more impartial in [his] prayers on such occasions" and that "in a public discussion each party must grant the possibility of himself being in the wrong and his opponent in the right, and that in our prayers this impartiality should be recognized, if for nothing else, as a matter of courtesy and consistency." And Holsinger accepted the correction!

The fact that someone as contentious as Holsinger could readily and graciously accept such correction says worlds about the respect in which Quinter was held by Holsinger and by the church at large during this turbulent time. While definitely progressive in many ways, Quinter's humble manner and understanding ways kept him in harmony with most of the Brotherhood; so much so that he was in great demand as a committee member at Annual Conference, serving as its assistant or writing clerk for 27 years.

Perhaps the best known incident in Quinter's life came at its very end—appropriately surrounded by the Brethren at Annual Conference. On May 19, 1888, in North Manchester, Ind., Quinter died while on his knees leading prayer at the close of Saturday afternoon worship. His final words were "We are glad to meet again." A historical marker can be found near the Peabody Retirement Community commemorating these final, most fitting words of this humble and beloved Dunker educator, publisher, and preacher.

Polarization and schism among the Brethren

by Kenneth M. Shaffer Jr.

Three-way split "rent the Brethren fabric" in the early 1880s

A petition to the 1880 Annual Meeting called for the removal of "the fast element from among us, which is the cause of the troubles and divisions in the church."

The petition, generally known as the Miami Valley Petition, came from a group of elders in southern Ohio; those supporting the petition became known as the Old Order group. While the petition condemned the "fancy painting" of houses and barns, "fine furniture," and "costly carriages," the major opposition was to innovations such as: (1) education in high schools and colleges, which were unsafe places for simple Christians; (2) Sunday schools that usurped the duty of parents; (3) revival meetings where revival songs were sung and invitations given; (4) the salaried ministry where ministers were paid to preach the gospel; and (5) the single mode of feetwashing where one person washes and dries the feet of a neighbor and the neighbor in turn washes and dries the feet of the next person. The petition provided biblical texts to explain why each of the five innovations was not in accordance with the gospel.

The "fast element" referred to in the petition was the Progressive group. Progressive Brethren advocated the very things the Old Orders opposed. In addition, the Progressives and Old Orders disagreed on evangelism and foreign missions. The Progressives favored both, and the Old Orders opposed both. Neither group, however, was pleased with Annual Meeting. For the Progressives Annual Meeting tried to exercise too much authority; for the Old Orders Annual Meeting did not enforce its decisions strictly enough.

There were divisions before the early 1880s, and there were divisions after. But, as Donald Durnbaugh says: **"Nothing approached the trauma of this three-way split of the early 1880s."**

The Progressives presented their positions in publications such as *The Christian Family Companion* (1865-1875) and *The Progressive Christian* (1878-1883). According to Henry Holsinger, who published both papers, the purpose of *The Christian Family Companion* was "to remove certain hindrances to the prosperity of the church....One of these hindrances was called 'avoidance.'"

Avoidance was the practice whereby the church did not associate with those members who refused to repent when disciplined for not living according to the principles of the Brethren. Another hindrance was the lack of educated ministers. Concerning *The Progressive Christian,* Holsinger said it was begun with "the avowed purpose of advocating progressive measures and reforms."

The majority of Brethren in the early 1880s were somewhere between the Old Orders and the Progressives. Many supported some Progressive reforms but wanted change to take place slowly. Some were offended by the in-your-face nature of articles that appeared in Progressive publications. For example, in 1879 an article titled "Is the Standing Committee a Secret Society?" appeared in *The Progressive Christian*. The article listed similarities between the Annual Meeting Standing Committee and secret societies. At that time Brethren were forbidden to join secret societies, such as Free Masons and Odd Fellows, on the basis of John 18:19-24.

When the Miami Valley Petition came to the 1880 Annual Meeting, it was replaced by a substitute paper written by the Standing Committee. This substitute paper, which sought to be conciliatory, was approved. It acknowledged the Old Orders' concerns but did not condemn the innovations.

The Old Orders were particularly offended by the last paragraph of the substitute paper, which called for "forbearance" on the issue of feetwashing. Members were advised "to allow the same liberty of conscience for brethren that we ask for ourselves" when it came to the mode of feetwashing. The Old Orders did not feel they had been heard and so resubmitted their petition, with a few changes, to the 1881 Annual Meeting. This time the petition was rejected because it did not come through a district meeting.

At this point the Old Orders gave up. They decided Annual Meeting was never going to put a stop to the progressive ideas and practices developing in some congregations. At an August 1881 meeting, they adopted resolutions that stated why they could not remain with the larger body of Brethren. While the resolutions named the specific areas of disagreement, the overall problem, as they saw it, was that the church was "fast drifting into the popular customs of the world." In December 1881 they organized as the Old German Baptist Brethren.

The withdrawal of the Old Orders did not bring harmony to the main body of the church. The Progressives were still pressing for reforms, and they were becoming impatient. Holsinger, their acknowledged leader, tended to be a harsh critic when calling for change. When calling for an educated ministry, Holsinger described the elders as "incompetent bishops."

Eventually Holsinger became the focal point of the Progressive movement. Five districts presented charges against him at the 1881 Annual Meeting, the same meeting that refused to reconsider the Miami Valley Petition. These charges were based on articles he published that were considered contrary to Brethren beliefs and practices. As a result, a committee was sent by Annual Meeting to visit Holsinger in Berlin, Pa., to "deal with him according to his transgressions." This became known as Holsinger's trial, but no actual discussion of the transgressions took place because of disagreements about who could attend the meeting and whether the proceedings could be recorded.

The committee recommended to the 1882 Annual Meeting that Holsinger be disfellowshipped; the recommendation, after long discussion, was approved. During the following year the Progressives held meetings and wrote documents presenting their viewpoint. However no official separation took place, because there was still hope for reconciliation at the 1883 Annual Meeting. But no reconciliation was forthcoming, and in June 1883 the Progressives organized the Brethren Church.

The majority of Brethren in the early 1880s were **somewhere between the Old Orders and the Progressives.** Many supported some Progressive reforms but wanted change to take place slowly.

In the aftermath of the divisions, individuals and congregations were sometimes faced with a difficult choice. With which of the three groups would they identify? Some congregations split, and disputes arose over property. In a few instances there were lawsuits. Eventually, in the 20th century, the three groups began to cooperate on some projects. Notable is the work of the *Brethren Encyclopedia Board*, which includes representatives from all three groups plus several other Brethren groups.

In 1983, 100 years after the divisions, the board published the three-volume *Brethren Encyclopedia*, followed by a fourth volume in 2005. The board has published other books and organized four Brethren World Assemblies. Also notable is the cooperation between the Brethren Church and the Church of the Brethren that has occurred in foreign mission work, disaster relief, and evangelism. In 2008, the Brethren Church and the Church of the Brethren held their annual conferences concurrently in Richmond, Va.

A question often raised is why did the divisions of the early 1880s occur? Obviously there were specific issues (higher education, paid ministry, mode of feetwashing, etc.), but why did these become issues among Brethren? Several answers to this question have been suggested. The answer favored by this writer is that the Brethren had to decide how to respond to the change taking place in the larger society.

In the years following the Civil War, the United States experienced remarkable economic growth and social change. The country was moving from an agricultural society to an industrial society. Three different responses to these changes developed among the Brethren. One group (the Old Orders) wanted to resist change, especially if it meant changing the traditional ways of the church. Another group (the Progressives) wanted to embrace change, especially new methods being adopted by other denominations. A third group (the Church of the Brethren of today) wanted to change slowly. At the 1880 Annual Meeting, they said of themselves: "While we are conservative, we are also progressive."

There were divisions before the early 1880s, and there were divisions after. But, as Donald Durnbaugh says: "It was not until the last half of the nineteenth century that schism completely rent the Brethren fabric.... Nothing approached the trauma of this three-way split of the early 1880s."

Sources: *Fruit of the Vine* by Donald F. Durnbaugh; *Holsinger's History of the Tunkers and The Brethren Church* by H. R. Holsinger; *The Brethren in Industrial America* compiled and edited by Roger E. Sappington; "Division Among the German Baptist Brethren" by Kerby Lauderdale; *The Brethren Encyclopedia; Brethren Life and Thought*, Summer 1979; Annual Meeting Minutes.

In mission in India

by Pamela K. Brubaker

Work began with orphanages and expanded rapidly

The Church of the Brethren mission field in India was opened in January 1895 by Wilbur B. and Mary Emmert Stover and Bertha Ryan (Shirk). The first mission station was at Bulsar, north of Bombay (now Mumbai) in western India.

By 1897 other missionaries had arrived, and expansion began. In 1899 mission stations were started at Anklesvar and Jalalpor. Other mission stations opened at Dahanu (1902), Vali-Umalla (1904), Vada and Vyara (1905), Ahwa (1907), and Palghar (1921). The mission encompassed a vast area, more than 7,000 square miles. Protestant missions in India practiced comity, which meant they did not overlap each other's area of work. Thus Brethren were the only Protestant group in this area.

During the early years of the mission, parts of India were suffering from severe famine, leaving many children orphaned. In 1897, 50 orphans were brought to an improvised house in Bulsar. Bertha Ryan was their supervisor. Of 13 persons baptized there on April 3, 1898, seven were orphans. Wilbur B. Stover and many others assisted in bringing destitute children to mission stations. In 1899 an orphanage and missionary residence were constructed at Bulsar. By that time orphan groups had also gathered at Anklesvar and Jalalpor.

Serving human needs and spreading the gospel were goals of the mission program from the beginning. Service and training institutions were crucial to growth. Elementary schools, training schools, and medical facilities followed the orphanages. Boys and girls boarding schools and hostels were founded at several stations. The Bulsar Bible Training School was established in 1912. Hospitals

Early Brethren missionaries to India gather for a photo on the steps of an orphanage in January 1905.

I.S. Long / Courtesy of Brethren Historical Library and Archives

were constructed at Bulsar in 1916 and Dahanu in 1925. Anklesvar saw the opening of a Vocational Training School in 1924 and a Rural Service Center in 1952. These institutions made significant contributions to education, health care, and agriculture, as did other Christian mission programs in India and elsewhere.

In the early years, this work was directed by missionaries. Many single women served on the mission field, along with married couples. Brethren church policy said that in preparation for the mission field there was "no discrimination as to the young people, whether they are brethren or whether they are sisters, or both, or whether they are in office." Men were expected to be "in the ministry"; for women "there is nothing of that kind in the way." Women served as educators, evangelists, nurses, and doctors.

Bertha Ryan represented the district of India at the 1900 Annual Meeting, the first recorded woman delegate. She spoke about "India's Call Upon the Church Today" at a pre-conference missionary meeting. Her speech focused on the needs of India, especially suffering from famine, diseases, and the condition of women.

During the early years of the mission, **parts of India were suffering from severe famine,** leaving many children orphaned. In 1897, 50 orphans were brought to an improvised house in Bulsar.

She concluded with a call to members of the church in the US to support both foreign and home missions.

In 1945, the Church of the Brethren in India became an autonomous church. At that time, there were 22 congregations with over 8,000 members. After India's independence in 1947, Indian church leadership developed quickly, and fewer overseas missionaries were needed. In 1970 the Church of the Brethren in India united with five other denominations to form the Church of North India. At that time, there were 20 evangelistic centers, 25 congregations, and about 18,000 people, including children, associated with the Brethren mission program.

The Church of the Brethren in the United States currently maintains ties with both the Church of North India (CNI) and the Church of the Brethren in India, established by some historic and new congregations that wish to be independent.

A DUNKER GUIDE TO BRETHREN HISTORY

1908-1958
Into all the world

Courtesy of Brethren Historical Library and Archives

From 1908 to 1958: The Brethren movement blossomed even as it experienced some growing pains. The image above is from the denomination's 200th anniversary celebration in Des Moines, Iowa, in 1908.

I.N.H. Beahm
'Little Man' with a big heart

by Anna M. Speicher

Isaac Newton Harvey Beahm was born in 1859 at Good's Mill, Va., near Bridgewater. He is probably best known today as the "Little Man" from the Brethren Press children's story by Dorothy Brandt Davis. But I.N.H., or "Brother Beahm," as he was often called, is still remembered by an older generation as a minister, educator, and tireless Brethren evangelist.

As a young man, I.N.H. worked as a farmhand, shoemaker, and wheelwright. Baptized in 1879, he was called to the ministry in 1881 and ordained as an elder in 1904. He enrolled at Bridgewater College in 1884 and was valedictorian of his graduating class in 1887. After a short stint as principal of schools in Bonsack, Va., he was called to join the faculty at Bridgewater in 1888. The teaching load was quite different then than it is today; in the two years he served at Bridgewater he taught nine subjects, including elocution, rhetoric, psychology, and arithmetic. In 1890 he married one of his students, Mary G. Bucher.

I.N.H. Beahm had a lifelong commitment to education at a time when many Brethren were skeptical about secular schooling. He not only taught but helped

> Brother Beahm was a staunch proponent of conservatism and maintaining a "set apart" Brethren identity.... **But unity of the body was more important to I.N.H. Beahm than traditionalism.**

found numerous schools at the high school and college level: Botetourt Normal College (later Daleville Academy); Prince William Normal School in Brentsville, Va.; and Hebron Seminary in Nokesville, Va. He moved to California to serve as president of Lordsburg College (now La Verne) in California, although he left the college after only a few months because of an illness then described as "neurasthenia." He was one of the early presidents of Elizabethtown College. A ministerial colleague once commented that I.N.H. Beahm "did more to make education acceptable in the Church of the Brethren than any single individual."

Brother Beahm also traveled widely as an itinerant preacher. This was not a very lucrative position, but I.N.H was committed to simple living as well as to his ministry. When one of his sisters paid a tailor to make him a good suit, he went to the tailor and asked for the money, telling the tailor that he needed the money more than he needed the suit. He then gave the money to a struggling congregation. In other cases, he borrowed money to assist churches.

His generosity toward others meant that he often had little for himself and his increasing family. On January 9, 1895, he wrote in his diary: "Father dines with us and I sit on Annie's high chair, eat from a tin pot lid and use a paring knife and a spoon for my knife and fork. It is cheap to be poor but unhandy." His daughter Mary said that they used to accuse their father of "tithing for the family and giving the balance to the Lord's work." Two of his six children later became well-known figures themselves in the Church of the Brethren: Anna Beahm Mow was a missionary, minister, teacher, author, and beloved speaker for many years; William Beahm was a missionary, teacher, and dean of Bethany Seminary from 1944 to 1962.

Brother Beahm was a fixture at Brethren Annual Meetings for 60 years. According to his son-in-law Baxter Mow, I.N.H. had an "inexhaustible fund of native wit" that sometimes helped to relieve tension and restore good feelings. Baxter once commented that his father-in-law's wide reading and oratorical skills must serve him well, and

Courtesy of Brethren Historical Library and Archives

I.N.H. replied—he said, with a twinkle—"Yes, I have it all pretty well mastered, except for two points. . . . First, what to say; second, how to say it."

Brother Beahm was a staunch proponent of conservatism and maintaining a "set apart" Brethren identity. In 1888, when the denomination began to talk about changing its official name—"German Baptist Brethren" being deemed misleading—Brother Beahm spoke on behalf of the old-fashioned name "Dunker Brethren" as opposed to the more newfangled "Church of the Brethren." In 1941, he petitioned the denomination to withdraw its membership in the Federal Council of Churches, precursor to the present National Council of Churches of Christ.

But unity of the body was more important to I.N.H. Beahm than traditionalism. Baxter Mow commented that "when . . . schism threatened, Brother Beahm advised the minority to be content and to go along with the majority." Around the time of the Second World War, a new schism was threatened. Brother Beahm was invited to preach at a conservative Bible conference and, according to one of those present, it was expected that he would be the "Moses" to lead the group out of the "Egypt" of the Church of the Brethren. But when he got up to preach, what he said to the group of 500 to 600 present was: "Brethren, I know the significance of this meeting. I know why you have gathered, what you intend to do. I know why you invited Brother Beahm to come and preach. . . . I am here to preach to you, and tell you why I am staying with the Church of the Brethren and why I think you ought to."

Brother Beahm characterized himself as one "of fervency for the oneness and conservation of Brethren-ism." He is known for an unparalleled feat of preaching: on July 26, 1931, he celebrated his 50 years of ministry by traveling 200 miles throughout Virginia by train and preaching 20 half-hour sermons in different locations that day. At age 91, he was still traveling and preaching. On Nov. 11, 1950, he attended a love feast at Jones Chapel, Va., with the intention of preaching the next day in a new church in Spray, N.C. But the car in which he was riding that night was struck by another driver; I.N.H. Beahm was thrown from the car and died instantly. Various tributes to Brother Beahm noted that this venerable preacher had always said that he wanted to die with his boots on—and that is what he did.

Sources: *The Brethren Encyclopedia*; I.N.H. Beahm, "Twenty Reasons on the Federal Council"; Carl Bowman, *Brethren Society*; Baxter M. Mow, "I.N.H. Beahm" and "A Tribute to I.N.H. Beahm"; Dorothy Garst Murray, *Sister Anna*; John W. Wayland, *Men of Mark and Representative Citizens of Harrisonburg and Rockingham County, Virginia.*

1908-1958

Ringing in
the bicentennial

by Frank Ramirez

1908 Annual Meeting brought a name change

The acoustics weren't great, the speakers read long addresses from manuscripts, and it's not clear if anybody was selling ice cream, but the Bicentennial Annual Conference proved to be an exciting event for Brethren who traveled all the way out to Des Moines, Iowa, June 3-11, 1908. *Gospel Messenger* editor J.H. Moore delivered his account in breathless paragraphs printed in two installments in the June 13 and June 20 issues that year.

Attendance was less than anticipated; even so, in addition to the 414 delegates there were more than 7,000 Brethren present! Unlike today, the moderator and other officers were not selected until the delegates had been seated. But some things would have been familiar to modern Conference-goers, such as the concern for good transportation between hotels and the conference center. On more than one occasion Moore praised the electric trains that shuttled the Brethren back and forth.

The 1907 Annual Meeting had recommended a committee that included two women be appointed to a planning committee, but only five men were selected, including such worthies as historian, educator, and future governor of Pennsylvania Martin Grove Brumbaugh; the world traveler D.L. Miller; famed preacher I.N.H Beahm; humanitarian and missionary S.N. McCann; and the neglected historian G.N. Falkenstein.

The essays they commissioned were presented at Annual Meeting and published as *Two Centuries of the Church of the Brethren: or the Beginnings of the Brotherhood*. This book, along with John Lewis Gillin's *The Dunkers: A Sociological Interpretation*, the massive *Literary Activity of the German Baptist Brethren in the Eighteenth Century* by John S. Flory, and John Walter Wayland's *The German Element of the Shenandoah Valley of Virginia*, were all meant to establish that the founders were all extremely educated men, and that no church had wielded as great an influence as the Brethren on Colonial America. (All four books can be obtained for free on the Internet through Google Books).

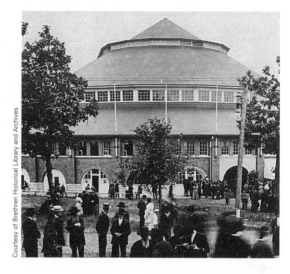
Courtesy of Brethren Historical Library and Archives

The packed 1908 agenda included one item that has had lasting influence: The official name of the denomination was changed from German Baptist Brethren to the Church of the Brethren, by a two-thirds voice vote.

"So far as we could learn" Moore wrote, "the decision of the Conference on this point gives excellent satisfaction. And now, since the question is settled, we should leave it settled. It is one of the things that cannot be changed every few years without serious consequences."

Moore's confident prediction that Annual Meeting would soon become primarily concerned with Christian education and missions work, and that the time spent on queries and church problems would diminish, has not been fulfilled.

The food, a feature always important to Brethren at Conference, earned high praise. A new twist was the additional presence of a newfangled cafeteria. The idea of entering without paying, selecting dishes priced at five cents each, and paying upon exiting was something novel to the editor. "Our people take to the idea quite readily," he noted.

Two Centuries of the Church of the Brethren made it into print during the bicentennial year, and although some of the articles may seem dated, "The Higher Spiritual Life of the Church" by Albert Cassel Wieand probably preserves the essence of how Brethren past, present, and hopefully future balance revelation and experience.

It states: "Practically, then, if we wish to grow in the ability to discern and enjoy the guidance of God we must set ourselves with all diligence, in the first place, to study the Bible to discover and understand the eternal and universal principles of righteousness which must control our lives.

"In the second place we must see to it that the Holy Spirit has full sway in our hearts, and that we never grieve nor quench nor hinder him in the least, nor shrink back when he would lead us on." Amen.

Brethren and the Pandemic

by Frank Ramirez

Influenza outbreak killed millions around the world

The year 1918 was a tough time to be Brethren. Prior to the America's entry into the Great War the leaders had confidently assumed their non-resistant stand would be respected by the government and society. After all, there had been tremendous resistance in the culture at large against entering what was seen as a European conflict. But the sentiment expressed in songs like "I Didn't Raise My Boy To Be a Soldier," which was a hit song in 1915, melted away when the United States entered the war in 1917.

Overnight, German-Americans forgot their German, flags suddenly made their way into sanctuaries, the National Anthem became a fixture before ballgames, and Brethren became the object of persecution, especially in the military camps that sprang up overnight. Some were tortured and killed. Forced to choose between compliance, noncombatant service, and total resistance against service, Brethren men turned to their leaders—who punted! The Brethren met in January 1918 in Goshen, Ind., drafted what came to be known as the Goshen Statement, then repudiated it when the government threatened to jail Brethren leaders.

Yet the greatest danger to Brethren in the camps, as well as in the churches, had nothing to do with the fighting. As the war wound to a bloody close, the Pandemic of 1918-1919, known in that era as the Spanish Influenza, killed up to 675,000 in the United States and up to 100 million people worldwide, far more than the conflict that preceded it. Death was dramatic and sudden, beginning with a dull headache that gave way to shivering, delirium, and semi-consciousness. The feet turned black, the face turned purple, with death caused by drowning as the patient's lungs filled with blood.

More than 25 percent of the population of the United States contracted the flu as it swept through large cities, as well as military camps where soldiers were

> **Brethren writers such as Julia Graydon, Rose D. Fox, and Alice Trimmer addressed not only the pandemic but the important pastoral opportunities that accompanied the disaster, setting a tone for the rise of women in ministry among the Brethren.**

crowded in close quarters.

Nor did the Angel of Death pass over Brethren enclaves. Churches were closed for weeks or even months. Love feasts were cancelled. Colleges were shut down. The obituary pages of *The Gospel Messenger* swelled as many died. Yet judging from the front pages of that periodical you would never have known that one of the Four Horsemen of the Apocalypse had descended in their midst! There were numerous articles on the war, the Armistice, on missions, and on the Forward Movement in Sunday Schools, but all references to the pandemic were relegated to the "Round Table" columns, obituaries, and correspondent sections inside the periodical. These included one mistaken news item early in the pandemic that reported those who abstained from alcohol were safe from the flu. Experience quickly proved that false.

By and large, articles about the flu were not written by the male elders of the church, but by women. Brethren writers such as Julia Graydon, Rose D. Fox, and Alice Trimmer addressed not only the pandemic but the important pastoral opportunities that accompanied the disaster, setting a tone for the rise of women in ministry among the Brethren.

The pandemic was at the divide between failure and change. The failure was that of the old guard who failed to provide counsel and support for young Brethren men in the military camps. Following the pandemic, Brethren experienced a shift in mission philosophy from an emphasis on evangelism to one of service, along with a growing ecumenicity, an increasing role for women in ministry, the rise of the professional ministry, as well as an intentional increase in cooperation between church and state that gave greater opportunities for conscientious objectors to serve God and humanity rather than take part in war. The flu may have been one of the factors that led to the Brethren Service explosion of the 1930s and '40s.

1908-1958

Caught off guard
at Goshen

by Steve Longenecker

**Brethren recanted anti-war statement
under threat of sedition charge**

Only once in 300 years did an immediate crisis require **Brethren** to convene as a denomination prior to their next annual gathering. During World War I a national draft of men into military service jeopardized Brethren pacifists, and the denomination responded with an emergency meeting in Goshen, Ind.

Conscription caught the denomination unprepared. The World War I draft was the nation's first in several generations, and at that point only the third in American history. Except for the Civil War and the Revolutionary War, volunteers had fought all other conflicts.

The new draft law gave conscientious objectors (CO's) few options. Regulations required all men between the ages of 18 and 45 to register and provided no opportunity for them to indicate CO status. Draftees who were CO's

Henry C. Early served as moderator of the Church of the Brethren in 1918.

had to report to military camp first, then declare their intent. But as CO's arrived, authorities were reluctant to accept their word, and documentation of their beliefs became essential. Moreover, Brethren draftees and the ministers who visited them complained that authorities treated CO's roughly.

Additionally, unforeseen philosophical questions arose regarding the Brethren relationship to conscription. Was the draft system itself sinful, even if CO exemption ultimately resulted? Could Brethren even register for the draft, or should they refuse to cooperate? Could Brethren accept government-run alternative service, or should the denomination administer the program? Was noncombatant status acceptable? Could noncombatants wear a uniform? Confusion reigned.

Many called for clarity. Accordingly, 400 Brethren gathered on Jan. 9, 1918, at Goshen in an extra meeting that had no standing in Brethren polity. Inviting delegates on short notice from each congregation was unrealistic, so Standing Committee, the Peace Committee, and pastors who had visited military camps comprised the 100-member delegate body. They passed a strong statement advising young men to "refrain from wearing the military uniform" and to avoid drilling and other military activities. The statement became a pamphlet used by Brethren CO's to verify their scruples.

When the War Department saw the Goshen document, authorities summoned W.J. Swigart and J.M. Henry, members of the Central Service Committee, to Washington, D.C. Authorities were upset because the Brethren at Goshen had discouraged participation in the military. The government recognized the right of individual conscience but not the right to express it. The War Department, therefore, threatened Swigart and Henry with sedition, which carried a lengthy prison sentence. Other opponents of the war had been jailed, and the warning was real.

Under pressure, the Brethren leaders repudiated the Goshen doctrine. Government officials went over the Brethren statement line by line with the denominational representatives before agreeing to it. Swigart had always favored noncombatant service ("that is all we ask"), and Henry claimed that at Goshen he had denounced the majority viewpoint as treasonous. Perhaps that made their recantation easier.

Justifying the new policy, Swigart explained in the *Gospel Messenger* that a "man is entitled to his opinion" and to practice it, but "he is not always at liberty" to express it or to "urge his conscience on others."

Score one for Big Brother.

THE SEDITION ACT

"Whoever when the United States is at war, shall willfully cause or attempt to cause, or incite or attempt to incite, insubordination, disloyalty, mutiny, or refusal of duty, in the military or naval forces of the United States, or shall willfully obstruct or attempt to obstruct the recruiting or enlistment services of the United States . . . shall be punished by a fine of not more than $10,000 or the imprisonment for not more than twenty years, or both." —excerpt from The Sedition Act of 1918, an amendment to the Espionage Act of 1917. The acts were repealed in 1921.

Dan West
Pied piper for peace

by Denise Kettering

Brethren 'visionary' helped to begin several major programs

I discovered many treasures while working at the Brethren Historical Library and Archives. In the bottom of an old filing cabinet, for example, I found a flute in a moldy, black case that once belonged to Dan West.

It seems an apt symbol for West's leadership. Like the legendary Pied Piper, Dan West played an original tune and led Brethren youth down a new path. Unlike the legend, however, he did not lead young people down the road to destruction; instead, he called youth to lives of peace, justice, and harmony. The song he composed while luring young men into alternative service, drawing young women into the camping movement, and inviting teenagers into peace education at times created strident notes within the denomination he loved.

Dan West's influence in the Church of the Brethren and around the world is itself legendary. Throughout the world, people have benefited from Heifer Project gifts, Brethren Volunteer Service (BVS), and education in peace studies

Dan West with his wife, Lucy.

programs. His extensive legacy cannot be fully described here, so instead consider three aspects of his life.

Courtesy of Brethren Historical Library and Archives

The music of peace
Born in 1893, West grew up in a Brethren home and attended both Bethany Bible School and Manchester College, so World War I presented the first real challenge to his Brethren ideals. His older half-brother, Pearl West, wrote to Dan on April 26, 1917: "You can avoid conscription by entering in arduous duties on the farm, but certainly I believe by entering the forest-service—if you do not wish to go to war."

Dan had begun to investigate alternatives to military service upon his graduation from Manchester, but in 1918 found himself drafted and installed at Camp Wadsworth, S.C., for training. In a letter to his brother Sam West on May 19, 1918, he wrote, ". . . the Co. Commander came by and asked if there were any COs (conscientious objectors). I think I was the only one in the company who stood up. It was a bit lonesome before that crowd who thot [thought] otherwise, but I didn't mind so much. . . . But I feel out of place here."

West's letters reflect his struggle with military service, even service as a noncombatant who taught soldiers basic reading, writing, and arithmetic skills. West's later concern with alternative service reflects his own interactions with the military and his desire to make sure other young men did not have to face military service.

The tune of justice
In 1937-1938 West traveled as a relief worker with the American Friends Service Committee to war-ravaged Spain. He wrote moving letters home to his wife, Lucy, about his experiences. On December 5, 1937, he wrote, "The hard part was having to refuse some of the needy who came in hope and went home empty-handed. It was very rough on me, but we had come to help the neediest only—not everybody. A few children poorly clad, with sores on their faces would have touched you deeply."

His daily missives to Lucy were full of stories about both the suffering and generosity of the people he met. He wrote on Oct. 7, 1937: "We were fed lunch . . . in an inn by one of the few families left in the little village and they would not take anything for a full course dinner for eight people! I didn't get many of their words, but I got the meaning—new evidence that I always meet good people everywhere I go." Clearly his famous quotation, "I will not eat cake as long as there are those in the world who don't have bread to eat," strongly reflected the horrors he witnessed in Spain.

Looking across the Spanish countryside, West noted its resemblance to his Indiana home, leading to his idea for the Heifer Project. If farmers in Indiana could supply the Spanish people with cattle, babies would no longer starve from lack of milk. He quickly put the idea to folks back in Indiana, and soon it turned into a denominational, interdenominational, and finally international organization, eventually becoming today's Heifer International.

In 1960, Dan and Lucy had the opportunity to travel across Europe and Asia. The trip was a triumphal moment for West, who had the opportunity to meet many people the Heifer Project had benefited. In his notes from the trip, he wrote a short reflection on justice in which he compared the American representation of blind justice holding scales to his alternate understanding of justice: "Justice has her eyes open to see, her hands free from both scales and sword—free to work." West's understanding of justice reflected his life philosophy: Look at the world with hands ready to serve.

The harmony of service
From 1927 to 1930, West traveled around the country with Perry Rohrer, Al Brightbill, and Chauncey Shamberger, breathing life into the camping movement. Years later, many Brethren men and women involved in West's discussion groups have remarked on the powerful impression he made on them during these years.

Looking across the Spanish countryside, West noted its resemblance to his Indiana home, leading to his idea for the Heifer Project. If farmers in Indiana could supply the Spanish people with cattle, babies would no longer starve from lack of milk.

Courtesy of Brethren Historical Library and Archives

Dan West, right, presents cattle as part of the "Heifer Project" he envisioned.

West took an official job with the denomination in 1930, using both his vision-ary potential and renegade spirit to create new youth and service programs. M.R. Zigler related about West, "His imagination was tremendous, he was hard to live with really." West often wanted to take the church in a more radical direction than the more pragmatic Zigler believed it was ready to go. Zigler respected West as a visionary, but maintained, "Dan was hard to live with because the way . . . he dressed, where he thought you ought to live, on the farm and down the line." West challenged others to live in a way that encouraged peace and justice in all aspects of life, making him a difficult model to imitate.

West's work with youth was influential in the formation of BVS and peace studies programs. He refused to present the idea for BVS to Annual Conference himself, but became a discussion leader for BVS training units during the pro-gram's inception. He also pushed Manchester College to begin a peace studies program, even teaching the first class, "A Basis for an Enduring Peace."

Annual Conference chose West as the 1966 moderator, the first non-ordained moderator of the Church of the Brethren. During his address, titled "Not to Destroy But to Fulfill," he urged Brethren to "select the best from Brethren and other heritages (the measure is always the mind of Christ) and bid steadily for the hearty cooperation of all other groups going our way." West respected

Brethren heritage, but also urged Brethren toward peace, cooperation, and harmony with other Christians to benefit the world.

Dan West left an indelible impression on the Church of the Brethren. He became a legend remembered by the young people he influenced and memorialized by the organization that he envisioned on a Spanish hillside. Zigler, in his eulogy at Dan West's funeral in 1971, stated, "If Dan West would have been born 10 years early, he couldn't have been Dan West that we know. If he had come 10 years later, he could not have been Dan West."

West arrived at the necessary moment in the Church of the Brethren. He played his tune of peace and justice for the people of the world and inspired generations of Brethren who willingly followed him in the path of service.

Sources: All quotations are taken from the Dan West Papers at the Brethren Historical Library and Archives in Elgin, Ill.

BVS IS BORN

Brethren Volunteer Service (BVS) began in 1948, when a group of young adults—encouraged by Dan West and others—proposed to Annual Conference an item no on the agenda: beginning a volunteer service program for the denomination Delegates approved it, and the first orientation unit was held just months later, i September 1948.

BVS provided alternative service placements during the Korean an Vietnam wars, and it began accepting conscientious objectors from German in 1968. Volunteers serve across the United States, in Europe, in Latin Americ and elsewhere.

BVS celebrated its 60th anniversary with a reunion gathering in Ne Windsor, Md., September 26-28, 2008.

Let's go camping

by Jane Davis

Outdoor ministry blossomed in first half of 20th century

Long recognized as an excellent teaching tool, camping began as early as 1823 in Massachusetts. The Fresh Air Movement (1872) raised awareness for the nation's poor in the ghettos and slums of the cities, while organized groups such as the YMCA began establishing campgrounds in rural areas. Soon, other religious groups considered camping and campgrounds.

Brethren expansion across the United States by 1908 led to district organizations, and district meetings involved travel time and expense. Families looked forward to attending these meetings for the spiritual and social aspects as well as business. In an effort to strengthen ties among district churches, activities for youth and adults were offered in rented campgrounds. Edgar Rothrock and Virgil Finnell organized a summer assemblies family camp for the Nebraska District (1917) that became an annual event.

Numerical growth allowed districts to purchase camp sites. Western Pennsylvania led the way with Camp Harmony (1923). A centralized, traveling leadership sponsored by the Board of Religious Education in Elgin, Ill., aided the growth of these summer camps, further enhanced by missionaries on leave from India, Africa, and other areas of service sharing their experiences and encouraging service work.

DID YOU KNOW?

There are 29 camps and outdoor ministry programs in the denomination today, stretching from the Pacific Northwest to Florida and from Pennsylvania to California.

Courtesy of Brethren Historical Library and Archives

Left to right, Perry Rohrer, Dan West, Chauncey Shamberger, and Al Brightbill made up "The Four Horsemen" who traveled to Brethren camps in the 1930s.

Later, Brethren Volunteer Service workers filled an important role in camping programs. District ministers and local church workers completed the leadership, acquainting local youth with others across the Brotherhood. Often time spent at camp became a turning point for campers, as many dedicated their lives to Christ, with baptism at camp or their home congregation. Camping brought a world view to the local campers, introduced them to new cultures, Brethren leaders, and missionaries, and created a mix of Brethren from across the Brotherhood. One camper later remarked that with leadership such as this at their camp, "We knew they were real people with hair on their arms like the rest of us."

The 1930s group known as the "four horsemen"—Dan West, director of Young People's Work; Perry Rohrer; Alvin Brightbill; and Chauncey H. Shamberger—traveled by auto from camp to camp during the summers. By the end of the 1930s Brethren had 15 permanent camps and had held 60 sessions with 6,280 campers attending. A brochure advertising the 1930 Young People's Conference at Camp Hillyard, near St. Joseph, Mo., contains a picture of 70 attendees at the 1929 conference. Worship, numerous discussion groups, informal time and recreation, a closing vespers, and campfire made up the day's activities.

The Great Depression and Dust Bowl days of the 1930s brought financial problems to camps in the Plains states. District leaders considered discontinuing camping, but youth in the Northern and Middle Missouri districts strongly believed camping should continue. A scrapbook containing photographs of activities, hand-drawn camp scenes in white India ink on black scrapbook sheets, names of campers and leaders, and courses taught at camp was presented to the district elders. Camping in the Missouri districts continued as families provided food for camp and other cost-cutting measures were implemented.

Growth in the camping program peaked with 12,058 campers in 1955 and 38 district camps in 1957. District mergers lessened the number of camps needed. Programs were implemented to meet the needs of the local districts and organizational changes in denominational structure. Winterized camping, year-round paid staff, historical tours, and outdoor education environmental classes for public school children are some of the newer offerings at Brethren camps today.

China revisited
A legacy of mission

by Gene Wampler

Brethren work began in the country in 1908

On July 30, 1908, while the newly renamed Church of the Brethren was celebrating its 200th anniversary, the vanguard of Brethren mission work in China—Frank and Anna Crumpacker with Emma Horning and George and Blanche Hilton—left Seattle on the *USS Minnesota*. Four weeks later they arrived in Shanghai and traveled to Taiyuan, capital of Shanxi province. There, with the help of Paul Corbin of the American Board mission, they investigated the possibility of establishing mission work in Shanxi.

After 2,000 years of government under the imperial system, China was in the midst of a century of turmoil. Western powers had opened treaty ports following the Opium War of 1839-1842. Now, in 1908, Shanxi province was still reeling from the 1900 debacle of the anti-Western, anti-Christian "Boxer" rebellion and the subsequent violent suppression by Western powers. All of the missionaries in Shanxi had either fled or been killed, and mission work was only slowly returning.

In April 1910 two young Chinese men, the first Brethren converts, were baptized. Later that year a Brethren mission station was established in Ping Ting, and on Sunday, June 12, the first public preaching service was held in the Crumpacker home with about 40 attending. By the following year the Hiltons had taken an early furlough for medical reasons and Minerva Metzger joined the group. On May 10, 1911, the first love feast was celebrated in the Crumpacker home with four Americans and three Chinese participating.

Six new missionaries arrived in September 1911 but had to remain in the coastal city of Tientsin along with the Shanxi workers who had evacuated to the same city. China was in the process of overthrowing the imperial government and establishing a republic. That revolution was successful, but the country remained unsettled as various Chinese factions struggled for control.

Despite the turmoil, Brethren returned to Shanxi in the spring of 1912 and the mission work grew. Schools and hospitals were established in Ping Ting, Liao Chou,

Courtesy of Brethren Historical Library and Archives

Mission meeting at Ping Ting, September 1912. The Chinese characters, from right to left, read "Ping Ting County Friend Love Society (Church of the Brethren) gathering."

and Shou Yang. Additionally, evangelistic centers were located in Taiyuan, Ho Shun, Ku Cheng, Ma Tien, Yu She, and Chin Chou. Major relief efforts were undertaken during the plague in the winter of 1917-1918 and the famines of 1912 and 1920. By 1929 there were 1,255 members in four congregations with one Chinese pastor and 42 paid evangelists. A student population of 644 was being educated in 14 schools. The outlook was very positive.

Open conflict between China and Japan began in July 1937 with the incident at Marco Polo Bridge near Peking (now Beijing), and conditions deteriorated rapidly. Since America was not yet at war with Japan, US citizens were on polite relations with the Japanese army. But missionaries were helping Chinese refugees and making it more difficult for the Japanese to assert full control. In December 1937, Alva and Mary Harsh and Minneva Neher disappeared, presumably killed by the Japanese. By late 1940 tension between the occupying Japanese and Brethren in Shanxi was extreme. In addition to the three missionaries, 13 Chinese Christians accused of spying were executed. In December, Chinese church leaders asked that the Americans leave, and plans were made to do that.

Six new missionaries had arrived in August 1940 and were in the Peking Language School. They, along with Lloyd and Ellen Cunningham, moved with the school to the Philippines in the spring of 1941 and spent the war in a Japanese internment camp. Three others who had chosen to remain in Peking were interned in China. The rest returned to America in early 1941.

Between 1908 and 1941, 83 Brethren had served in China and 12 lost their lives to that service, either in China or as the result of diseases contracted there.

Ernest Wampler and O.C. Sollenberger returned to lay the foundation for a Brethren Service medical/relief effort in "Free China" in September 1941. But America's entry into the war three months later prevented the rest of the group

Between 1908 and 1941, **83 Brethren had served in China and 12 lost their lives to that service,** either in China or as the result of diseases contracted there.

from going. Wampler and Sollenberger were able to coordinate some relief work with the American Advisory Committee and returned to America in July 1943.

After the war a strong contingent of missionaries returned to China. Brethren Service sent a group of "Plowboys" to help reclaim farmland, and a shipment of heifers was sent in 1946. But the developing Communist revolution limited work in Shanxi province, and the mission work was moved to southern China. This initiative was also stymied as the Communists advanced south, assuming full control of the mainland in 1949. The last Brethren missionary returned to the United States in 1951.

Very little physical evidence remains of the Brethren mission work. The hospital in Ping Ting has a memorial to the Brethren work there, recognizing that the Brethren had established the hospital, but none of the buildings remain. The church building in Liao Chou (now Zuoquan) is a restaurant. As I stood in the former pulpit area to take a picture, Wang Baotien (whose father, uncle, and cousin were killed by the Japanese) commented, "This is where your father baptized me, three times under the water." He had fought the Japanese during the war and risen to a middle-level administrator afterwards. His daughter credits his training in the mission schools for teaching him the qualities of honesty and fairness that gained him the trust and respect of his fellow workers.

What does remain of the work and sacrifice of more than 100 Brethren missionaries and Brethren Service workers? There are several answers.

First, lives of individual Chinese were changed. Souls were brought to Christ. The seed of Christianity was planted. The Christian Church in China is thriving. A former Methodist mission church served in recent years by Pastor Yin—son of Elder H. C. Yin, a leader in the Chinese Brethren church since 1912—now numbers 5,000 members. It is one of 10 Protestant churches in Beijing.

Not surprisingly, the situation in rural areas is very different from the large, cosmopolitan cities. Local government is more conservative and exercises stronger control than in the major cities. While Christian congregations exist, they keep a low profile.

Second, children were educated. When Communism came to China peasant children were the favored class, and those who had been educated in mission schools were better prepared for leadership. The influence of their Christian training remains today.

Third, lives were spared and made easier. In 1930 the three hospitals treated some 20,000 patients. Famine relief, plague control, and health education spared many thousands more. Missionaries who had been raised on farms interacted easily with farmers in central Shanxi province, introducing improved crop varieties, hybrid sheep, and an associated wool industry.

Finally, the status of women was greatly improved. Because educated men often left the village for opportunities in the cities, women played a major role in educating local communities and the next generation. Often the only person in a village who could read was a woman. Educated girls, wives, and mothers introduced a basic understanding of nutrition, child care, and health care, while small handicraft industries contributed to their economic stability.

ENCOUNTERS IN CHINA

In the summer of 2006, Joe and Gene Wampler led a family group back to Shanxi province and visited again the area where they were born and spent most of their early years.

Gene relates: "During a taxi ride in Beijing, as we passed the former mission compound, I mentioned to the driver that I had lived there in 1947. The driver said there was a church there. I said, 'I know, I used to attend that church.' Then I asked if he was a Christian and he said he was. He said that a lot of people attend that church; some understand the meaning and some do not. (I took him to mean that he did understand.)"

"The Brethren mission work and the missionaries themselves are fondly remembered," he adds. "In the village where Joe and I had

Remembering "Wang mushi" in Chin Chou, now Quinshen, during a visit in 2006.

spent our early childhood, Joe struck up a conversation with an old gentleman who was playing Chinese chess and mentioned he had lived there 70 years earlier. The gentleman said, '*Wang mushi*' ('Pastor Wampler'). Joe asked if he had known *Wang mushi* and the man replied, 'Everybody knew him and everybody loved him.' "

Into Africa
Ekklesiar Yan'uwa a Nigeria

by Janis Pyle

Nigerian church has more than 150,000 members

After initial mission efforts to Denmark (1876), India (1894), and China (1908), the Church of the Brethren felt called to Africa. The first Brethren worship service in Nigeria was held on March 17, 1923, by H. Stover Kulp and Albert D. Helser under a tamarind tree in the village of Garkida.

"Each of us prayed that this spot might be a fountain to which people might come and drink of the Water of Life and eat of the Bread of Life," Helser wrote. Although beset by personal tragedies, the missionaries began to translate the Scriptures into the local Bura language, engage in health care, and establish schools and a hospital. In the following decades, the Church of the Brethren Mission (CBM) continued to establish schools and other programs, and its influence spread from Garkida into new areas.

In 85 years, Ekklesiar Yan'uwa a Nigeria (EYN)—the Church of the Brethren in Nigeria—has grown to be the largest Church of the Brethren national body in the world, with more than 150,000 members in 1,000 churches. The energy and vitality of the membership has resulted in active evangelism and church planting efforts within Nigeria and recently to other neighboring countries. Continual pastoral leadership training is needed for this growing church, as 10 to 15 new congregations are formed annually.

Invitations to the US church to send teachers for key assignments have become areas for meaningful partnering in ministry. The following schools were begun and continue with Brethren vision and support:

• Kulp Bible College (KBC), near Mubi, is the major training institution for Nigerian church leadership with an enrollment of approximately 180 students;

Brethren in Nigeria hold an outdoor feetwashing service.

Don Mitchell

- the church-sponsored Comprehensive Secondary School, based on the KBC and EYN headquarters property;
- and Hillcrest School in Jos, a K-through-12 school started by the Church of the Brethren and now run by a consortium of missions, providing American-style education for the children of mission workers throughout West Africa.

Leadership development grants from the Church of the Brethren's Global Mission Partnerships office also support more than 200 people annually as they prepare for pastoral ministry, graduating 60 to 70 people each year for service in the church. The Theological Education by Extension program trains over 1,500 people annually in basic Brethren beliefs and practices and denominational history. The program results in a biblically grounded laity, and some graduates are prompted to consider pastoral ministry.

Active programs of wells, health care, and schools—central mission ventures since the beginning of mission work in Nigeria— have been handed over to the Nigerian church for direction and implementation. The Mason Technical School joined with a number of these ministries as the church adapted an integrated community development approach.

These church outreach ministries continue to assist communities in some of the more isolated areas of northeast Nigeria. And an annual workcamp continues to build strong relationships between the US and EYN churches.

1908-1958

Harold Snider
Flashes of
fundamentalism

by Tim Harvey

**Brethren joining Federal Council of Churches
spurs opposition**

Harold Snider was one of the most effective Brethren pastors in the first half of the 20th century. He was also one of the most controversial.

Born in 1900 in Waynesboro, Pa., Brother Snider was the pastor of two Church of the Brethren congregations: first in Martinsburg, W.Va., then in Lewistown, Pa., beginning in 1941. During his tenure as pastor, both congregations experienced significant growth. The Martinsburg church grew from a part-time to a full-time pastoral program during his tenure; the Lewistown congregation grew to have more than 800 members.

But in spite of his success as an evan-

DOES THE BIBLE SANCTION

WAR?

WHY I AM NOT
A PACIFIST

HAROLD SNIDER
LEWISTOWN, PA.

Foreword by HERBERT LOCKYER, D.D. Editor: The Christian Digest.

Courtesy of Brethren Historical Library and Archives

gelist, Brethren history remembers Harold Snider most for the controversy generated by his opposition to the Brethren joining the Federal Council of Churches (FCC)—a controversy that ultimately led to the division of the Lewistown congregation.

In 1941, the Brethren Joint Council of Boards sent a resolution to Standing Committee requesting membership in the FCC. This resolution had the backing of many ecumenically minded church leaders of the day, most notably M.R. Zigler. This ecumenical desire was born out of Brethren encounters with the widespread suffering caused by events leading up to World War II.

Brethren had served in many foreign fields in the 1930s and 1940s, and along with seeing much suffering they had encountered leaders of other Christian denominations doing similar work. The rationale for joining the FCC was to "give Protestantism a strong voice in the many strategic situations which now exist throughout the world" (Annual Conference Minutes, 1923-1944, p. 162). Delegates at the 1941 La Verne, Calif., Annual Conference overwhelmingly approved joining the FCC.

The decision angered ardent supporters of fundamentalism like Harold Snider. They saw the leaders of both the Church of the Brethren and the FCC as departing from the doctrines of true Christianity. Snider accused denominational leaders of forcing a controversial item of business through the La Verne Conference too quickly, and of not printing his own viewpoints in the *Gospel Messenger*. He accused the FCC of supporting modernism; of denying the inerrancy of the Scriptures; of economic plans that resembled socialism; and of seeking change through government action.

Because of his increasing frustration with Brethren leadership, Snider began publishing his own magazine. Beginning in 1945, Snider published *The Christian Beacon*, which was soon renamed *The Brethren Fundamentalist*. These publications fueled the fundamentalist debates of the 1940s, in large part to Snider's incendiary language. Brethren leaders were compared to "Stalin" and "Hitler," highly insulting names considering the recent events of World War II. When district and denominational leadership began to seek resolution to the controversy, they were accused of attempting to "purge" the denomination of fundamentalism.

These attempts to resolve the situation were unsuccessful. The controversy finally came to a head in 1948, when district leadership removed Snider's ministerial credentials and asked him to vacate the pulpit and the parsonage of the Lewistown church. Snider predictably refused, and attempted to take the congregation out of the Church of the Brethren. A minority of Lewistown members sought to remain with the Church of the Brethren, and the question of who had proper right to the church property was settled in court. The court awarded the property to the group who wished to remain faithful to the Church of the Brethren.

Snider took the rest of the congregation and formed Calvary Independent Church (renamed Calvary Bible Church), where he served as pastor until 1959. Harold Snider died in Arizona in 1993.

A DUNKER GUIDE TO BRETHREN HISTORY

1958-2008
Peace and possibilities

Courtesy of Brethren Historical Library and Archives

From 1958 to 2008: In a changing era for the church, beloved Brethren figures like Anna Mow and M.R. Zigler provided the voice of the denomination as the second half of the 20th century rolled on. They cast a vision and inspired a new generation of leaders to continue to make a mark in the world.

Anna Beahm Mow
A fount of inspiration
by J. Kenneth Kreider

Sister Anna was known for her insight and wit

In the early 1950s the district youth of eastern Pennsylvania held a weekend retreat at Camp Swatara. An Elizabethtown College co-ed whispered to another co-ed, "Have you seen the speaker for this weekend? This is going to be dull, boring."

Indeed, dressed in a plain black dress, black stockings, and white prayer covering, this short, stocky lady, Anna Mow, did not look terribly exciting to the teenagers. As she began speaking, an early illustration mentioned Elvis Presley; surprised, the youth wondered, "What does this lady know about Elvis?"

With inspiring anecdotes, comedy, and insight, this master communicator quickly had them all on the edge of their seats. Mesmerized by her intriguing, relevant, and inspiring message, the youth were astonished as the hour was quickly spent. One of the lessons learned was illustrated by the remark of the co-ed who had anticipated a boring hour: "Never again will I judge someone by their outward appearance."

Anna Beahm Mow was born on July 31, 1893, in Daleville, Va. Her parents were Isaac Newton Harvey (affectionately known as I.N.H. or Brother Beahm) and Mary Bucher Beahm. Her father was an educator and evangelist who traveled widely among the Brethren. He saw to it that she and her siblings received the best education available, including his own academic instruction. Her parents taught and lived a life of virtue, acceptance, and understanding. Her father, for example, never wanted to be dressed so nicely that he could not identify with the poorest parishioner in the congregation.

This standard was difficult for his young daughter to accept. When he informed his family that they would be moving from California to Pennsylvania, where he was chosen as the first principal and president of what would become Elizabethtown College, the 6-year-old Anna "cried and cried." Her father told her

Courtesy of Brethren Historical Library and Archives

Anna Beahm Mow speaks at the 1978 Annual Conference in Wichita, Kan.

that she would have to change her wardrobe, because the conservative Brethren in eastern Pennsylvania would never tolerate frilly petticoats on the daughter of a Church of the Brethren preacher and head of the new college. She made the necessary adjustments, excelled as a young student, and decided at an early age that her goal was to be a missionary to India. She earned degrees from Manchester College and Bethany Bible School, and married Baxter M. Mow, who held degrees from the University of Idaho, Bethany Bible School, and the University of Chicago. He was a Rhodes scholar to Oxford University and acquired knowledge of many languages, including Latin, Greek, Hebrew, Aramaic, German, French, Gujurati, Hindi, Hindustani (Urdu), and Arabic.

They both dreamed of service on the mission field in some distant land, but they were sent to the Blue Ridge Mountains of Virginia to carry out a "home mission" assignment. On a salary of $23 per month, they rented a log house for $1 per month. With no car, and living in a village 27 miles from the nearest railroad station, they were obliged to carry out their mission on foot. Their willingness to live on the same level as their neighbors contributed to their popularity and acceptance in that mountain community. Brethren will gain a true idea of poverty, dedication, sacrifice, and faith if they read the first two chapters of Dorothy Garst Murray's excellent biography of Anna, *Sister Anna* (Brethren Press, 1983).

After two years of dedicated service in Rappahannock County, Va., the Mows received a notice from the General Mission Board of the Church of the Brethren that there was an opening for them to go to India. Within a month, in October 1923, they arrived in Bombay. Their service in India coincided with the heroic efforts of the great Gandhi to achieve national independence from Great Britain by the seemingly unrealistic tactics of nonviolence and non-cooperation with the occupier.

Gandhi's philosophy of nonviolence and respect for the dignity of all individuals was quite radical in Indian society, which for centuries had lived with strict caste divisions. While radical for the established powers, these ideas fit quite comfortably with the background of the Mows, fresh from the mountains of Virginia and the teachings of the Brethren. Consequently, they became somewhat estranged from the majority of the foreign community living in India, but were accepted by the Indian community—both the untouchables and a few of the upper class.

Their three children were born during the early years of their service in India. While attending the missionary-operated boarding school at Woodstock, the Mow children became friends with the children of Vijaya Lakshmi Pandit, a sister of Prime Minister Nehru. From this a long-lasting friendship developed between Anna Mow and Madame Pandit.

After 17 years on the Indian mission field the Mows were dismayed to learn that political reasons caused the Indian government to refuse to renew their visa for further service in India. India's loss was gain for the Church of the Brethren. From 1940 to 1958, "Sister Anna" taught courses in Christian education, missions, and biblical studies at Bethany Biblical Seminary. Her students were impressed by her knowledge, wisdom, and "common sense," accompanied by her radiant sense of humor (sometimes referred to as "holy hilarity"), and ability to convey the love of God with insight and humility.

Anna and Baxter Mow on the mission field in India.

Her hectic schedule of teaching and family duties also included scholarship. She authored 10 books that had wide appeal, as they sold by the tens of thousands. *Say Yes to Life* was her first book; nearly 50,000 copies were sold. Even more popular, her second book—*Your Child from Birth to Rebirth*—was dedicated to "Concerned Parents and Teachers of Children." Translated from English into three other languages, worldwide sales exceeded 78,000. Her third book spoke to teenagers and young people; *Going Steady with God* went to 14 printings and more than 47,000 copies.

Sister Anna was one of the first women ordained in the Church of the Brethren and was a popular preacher and evangelist. She served her denomination on the General Board and on Annual Conference committees. Service for 10 years on the evangelism committee of the Federal Council of Churches (later called

National Council of Churches of Christ in the USA) illustrated her dedication to ecumenical cooperation with Christians of other persuasions.

Not only was her teaching an electrifying influence on many of the future leaders of the church, but also her home was known as a sanctuary of fellowship for people from all over the world. E. Stanley Jones and Madame Pandit were only two of the multitude of "citizens of the world" who enjoyed the hospitality of the Mow home.

Madame Pandit visited with Sister Anna in Chicago before going to Washington to present her credentials as India's ambassador to the United States. Madame Pandit also represented her country as ambassador to the Soviet Union, Mexico, and Ireland, and as the first female president of the United Nations General Assembly. Sister Anna was asked to look after the three Pandit daughters while they attended college in the United States. Madame Pandit once wrote, "Anna Mow is perhaps my dearest foreign friend. I have gained enormously by her friendship and have been sustained by her love. I've also learned a little humility from her."

In addition to her teaching, preaching, writing, running a home, and raising a family, Sister Anna was in constant demand as a lecturer and discussion leader for retreats, weekend institutes, camps, seminars, and training sessions. Those who were privileged to hear her will never forget her contagious and bubbling enthusiasm, her simple, down-to-earth illustrations, practical logic, solid personification of Christian love toward all people, infectious humor, and her spontaneous, unique, and distinctive laughter (sometimes lovingly referred to as a "cackle").

A missionary to India; friend of a national leader of India; seminary professor; author; delightful, entertaining, and inspiring lecturer; along with being a devoted wife and mother, Sister Anna's life has been summarized as the "story of a Christian life joyously, bravely, and perceptively lived."

Anna Beahm Mow was one of the great leaders of the Church of the Brethren. Her inspiring insights and infectious joy of life were an inspiration to thousands. Sister Anna's rich and full life on this earth ended on July 7, 1985; her dynamic Christian influence, however, will last indefinitely.

DID YOU KNOW?

Bridgewater (Va.) College sponsors an annual Anna B. Mow Lecture Series. . . . A recent book published by Bethany Theological Seminary, *The Something-Else Lady*, tells the story of Anna Mow. It is written by Earle Fike Jr. and illustrated by Mow's great-granddaughter Yolanda Wenger. . . . Mow is also remembered in Andy and Terry Murray's song, "Sister Anna, Beauty Queen."

M.R. Zigler
A crusader for peace
by J. Kenneth Kreider

**Legacy includes Brethren Service
Center in New Windsor**

W hen will Christians stop killing their fellow Christians?" thundered M.R. Zigler, as he spoke to countless congregations, district conferences, international assemblies, and Annual Conference delegates. He constantly chided, prodded, and encouraged Brethren and fellow Christians to put their professed faith and standard of conduct in the teachings of the Prince of Peace rather than in secular national leaders and nationalism.

Michael Robert Zigler (M.R., as most called him) was born Nov. 9, 1891, in the ancestral Zigler homestead, called the Tunker House, in Broadway, Va. The Tunker House—also significant as the site of the 1832 Brethren Annual Meeting and the former home of outstanding 19th-century Brethren writer and theologian Peter Nead—is commemorated as a historic landmark by both state and national registers. It is located just across the road from the home of another Brethren patriarch, John Kline, who was martyred during the Civil War.

Growing up in this historical setting, M.R. became firmly rooted in Brethren values and beliefs, especially those of peace and nonviolence. These views were reinforced at Bridgewater College, where he considered mission work, became head of the campus Young Men's Christian Association (YMCA), and was elected president of his graduating class (1916). He accepted the offer of free tuition, room, and board at Vanderbilt University's School of Religion.

During M.R.'s first year of study at Vanderbilt the United States entered World War I. He enlisted in the YMCA to participate in the Y's program of providing spiritual guidance for the thousands of young men pouring into military camps. After a few months of training, Zigler was assigned to Parris Island, the United States Marine Corps training camp in South Carolina. Throughout his life he would refer often to this assignment as the impetus that solidified his ded-

Courtesy of Brethren Historical Library and Archives

M.R. Zigler converses with WCC official Dr. John Mackie.

ication to a lifetime as a crusader for peace.

In 1918 M.R. married his college sweetheart, Amy Arnold, a petite, quiet schoolteacher. She has been referred to as the "woman who stayed behind," as she created a solid home as "a refuge from the whirlwind of her husband's active public life." They had two children, Robert and Geraldine.

Although he always maintained that the Marines also desired peace (but used different tactics to achieve it), his experience at Parris Island convinced him that he needed to work through the church. In 1919 M.R. accepted the offer to become general secretary of Home Missions under the General Mission Board and chairman of the Home Missions Advisory Committee. Turning his back on a YMCA post in New York at a salary of $5,000 per year and free rent, Zigler felt the "call of the church" and moved to Elgin, Ill., for an annual salary of $1,500, out of which he had to pay $720 annually for rent.

As Home Missions secretary he personally visited practically every Church of the Brethren congregation in North America. Only 25 out of 1,100 congregations did not benefit from his inspiring presentations. Through these visits and his other work he became known as a denominational leader.

When World War II broke out, Zigler became chairman of the Advisory Committee for Conscientious Objectors and executive secretary of the Brethren Service Committee. He worked with the Mennonites and the Society of Friends to develop an alternative to military service, Civilian Public Service (CPS). M.R. was elected the first chair of CPS, which provided an alternative to military service for thousands of conscientious objectors.

M.R. spearheaded the 1944 Brethren Service Committee purchase of the campus of Blue Ridge College in New Windsor, Md. This center became the collection center for millions of dollars' worth of material aid for subsequent distribution to people in need all over the world.

He was also a driving force behind the formation of Church World Service (CWS), a combined effort of various denominations to alleviate suffering around

A Mennonite Central Committee poster bears a favorite quote from Brethren leader M.R. Zigler.

LET THE CHRISTIANS OF THE WORLD AGREE THAT THEY WILL NOT KILL EACH OTHER.

the world. The Brethren Service Center in New Windsor was the collection and shipping center of material aid for CWS and other relief organizations.

An ecumenical approach to service was characteristic of M.R. Zigler, who was also a participant at the first meeting of the World Council of Churches in 1948 in Amsterdam. The Church of the Brethren was thus one of the founding members of the approximately 150 denominations from all continents, a number that had doubled by 1980. For seven years (1954-1961) M.R. was a member of the prestigious WCC central committee, which met annually to supervise the policies and programs of the WCC. He continually pricked the consciences of the international churchmen by reminding them that wars would cease when Christians of one nation refused to kill fellow Christians of another nation. Although some Brethren were uneasy about denominational membership in the WCC, M.R. was a life-long and enthusiastic advocate of cooperation with all Christian groups in the ecumenical spirit.

In 1948 Zigler was appointed director of Brethren Service in Europe and made his headquarters in Geneva, Switzerland. As director he supervised Brethren Service projects in Germany, Austria, the Netherlands, Great Britain, Poland, Greece, Turkey, and Italy. These projects were staffed with idealistic young people who had joined Brethren Volunteer Service (BVS) to give two years of their lives serving others. Although these young people were inexperienced, naïve, and had varying degrees of ability to speak the native language, they received complete confidence, encouragement, and support from M.R. Zigler. At worship services, conferences, and meetings the volunteers were mesmerized and invigorated by his

DID YOU KNOW?

One of the main buildings on the Brethren Service Center campus in New Windsor is named Zigler Hall. . . . Historian Donald F. Durnbaugh wrote a biography of M.R. Zigler, titled *Pragmatic Prophet*. . . . Zigler's gravesite is in Broadway, Va., near John Kline's.

stimulating and inspirational speeches and leadership.

His official service to the church ended with the commemorations of the 250th anniversary of the founding of the Church of the Brethren in Schwarzenau, Germany, on Aug. 6, 1958. With hundreds of international visitors in attendance, Zigler presided over the dedication of the new Alexander Mack elementary school, which had been financed by a sizable donation from the Church of the Brethren. Aided by an interpreter, he interviewed a recipient of a heifer from Heifer Project. During the main worship service, he was especially exhilarated to be able to introduce his friend, W. A. Visser 't Hooft, first general secretary of the World Council of Churches, who delivered congratulatory greetings to the Church of the Brethren from the world body.

With the anniversary commemoration concluded, the Ziglers set off for a well-earned vacation. While driving in Sweden they were involved in a terrible automobile accident that took the life of his beloved Amy and the two people in the other vehicle. M.R. was in the hospital for 99 days before he could be released to return to the United States.

Unable to quietly retire, he began years of riding Greyhound buses all over the United States to visit friends and acquaintances of a lifetime—and to ask them to financially support his new idea for peace. The response was positive. In 1974 the first On Earth Peace Conference was held in New Windsor. Semi-annual conferences were held for years as people were inspired by M.R.'s leadership and vision. On Earth Peace sponsored peace academies and the printing of various books on Brethren history. Now an Annual Conference agency, it continues into the 21st century as an influential advocate of reconciliation and peace.

In addition to world peace, other life-long passions of M.R. included restoring relations among the Brethren bodies (who trace their origins back to Schwarzenau), and the publishing of a Brethren encyclopedia. Invited by M.R. Zigler to an unofficial meeting at the Tunker House in 1973, influential leaders of various Brethren bodies met, "shook hands," and learned to know each other. Out of this meeting developed cooperation between leaders representing the Church of the Brethren, The Brethren Church, the Fellowship of Grace Brethren Churches, Old German Baptist Brethren, and the Dunkard Brethren Church.

This group appointed eminent Brethren historian Donald F. Durnbaugh to be editor of *The Brethren Encyclopedia*. With contributions from more than 1,000 people from the various Brethren groups, the first two volumes were published in 1983. Seeing this achievement and knowing that the representatives of the Brethren bodies were meeting together regularly, publishing books on Brethren heritage, and planning for the future, M.R. died in peace in 1985.

Fighting
the war at home

by Logan Condon

**Brethren peace stance faced challenges
during Vietnam era**

H e was walking to class when the bullet hit him. The damage to his vertebrae and spine would cost him part of a lung and leave his legs permanently paralyzed. Others were not so lucky. Shortly after noon on Monday, May 4, 1970, Dean Kahler—along with 12 other Kent State University students—would become a victim in one of the most polarizing events of the era. Kahler, a member of the Church of the Brethren, was one of 13 wounded when National Guard troops opened fire on a rowdy group of students who had gathered to protest American involvement in the Vietnam conflict. Four of the 13 would not survive their wounds.

The incident at Kent State became a pivotal example of the duality of the Vietnam conflict. It had become a two-front war: a conflict between armed soldiers in Southeast Asia, and one of public opinion at home in the United States. This tension tore at America and its people from the mid-1960s until the fall of Saigon in April 1975.

As early as 1965, mere months into American involvement in the Vietnamese war, anti-war activists were staging marches, protests, and sit-ins. Gallup polls taken that year indicated a large minority were not satisfied with military intervention in a conflict on the other side of the world. By war's end in 1975, millions of Americans had voiced opposition to the combat in the form of strikes, protests, petitions, letters, marches, and literature. Those who resisted bloodshed in Southeast Asia ran the

For many Brethren, **speaking out against an unpopular war was not easy,** but they chose to suffer rather than betray their convictions.

gamut from students to clergy, and even some veterans who had served in Vietnam. The Brethren, as one of the Historic Peace Churches, added their official voice to those who spoke against war in numerous Annual Conference statements.

Brethren pacifists knew that seeking peace would not be easy. Civilian Public Service (and later Brethren Volunteer Service) had been successful as an alternative to mandatory military service during World War II. It had not, however, erased the memories of Brethren who were persecuted for their refusal to take up arms. Brethren pacifists remembered John Kline, killed for refusing to fight for either the North or South during the American Civil War, and the Brethren imprisoned for treason and sedition for refusing to participate in the First World War.

Dean Kahler would discover this persecution not long after his near-fatal shooting. Although he was registered as a conscientious objector, he had not been a part of the violent protest at Kent State. He was not among the students hurling insults and debris at the National Guardsmen. He was simply on his way to class. In the ensuing months, however, he received hate mail accusing him of being a communist sympathizer.

Brethren who actively protested the war were persecuted by their fellow Americans. In 1967, as protesters marched from Manchester Church of the Brethren to the campus of Manchester College in North Manchester, Ind., they were heckled by assailants who pelted them with eggs and rocks, attempting to knock the candles from their hands and prevent entry to the chapel, where the march was to conclude.

Courtesy of Brethren Historical Library and Archives

Church of the Brethren member Dean Kahler, shown shortly after the Kent State shootings in 1970, and later in 1992.

Courtesy of Brethren Historical Library and Archives

Brethren and others protest the imprisonment of Church of the Brethren member Ted Glick, who was sentenced to 18 months in federal prison for destroying his draft files in 1970. Glick was known as one of the "Harrisburg Eight."

J. Kenneth Kreider, a now-retired professor at Elizabethtown College, was treated harshly for his opposition to the conflict in Vietnam in 1965. Despite his assurance that his stance was not anti-American, but rather anti-violence, Kreider was verbally attacked by other members of the faculty, many of whom circulated a petition to have him fired. Parents of many students who supported American foreign policy contacted the college president, demanding that the professor be dismissed. He received angry letters, some addressed to "Comrade Kreider." One even offered to buy him a one-way ticket to Russia. One morning, the Elizabethtown campus awoke to find an effigy of Kreider hung from a tree by a rope.

Cold war tensions extended beyond the Brethren college campuses. In an effort to foster good relations between East and West, Brethren participated in a series of exchanges with the Russian Orthodox Church. In 1963 and 1967, the Brethren hosted Metropolitan Nikodim and a delegation of Orthodox clergy. They visited the Brethren Service Center in New Windsor, Md., the General Offices in Elgin, Ill., and individual congregations across America. The visits were picketed by Americans who accused the Orthodox clergy of being Soviet agents and their hosts, W. Harold Row and M.R. Zigler of the Brethren Service Commission, of being communist sympathizers.

Some Brethren chose to make a much more public statement by refusing to register for the draft. Among them were Robert Gross and Larry Anderson, both convicted and sent to prison. In 1973, Anderson spent 19 weeks in jail, during which time his father took up the mantle of peace activism, coauthoring an Annual

> **Chandler Edwards,** who trained with a Brethren Volunteer Service unit, was killed shortly after delivering supplies to a Laotian village in April 1969. Two years later, **Ted Studebaker** was gunned down by the Vietcong as he worked on an agricultural project with Vietnam's mountain people.

Conference query supporting a World Peace Tax Fund and taking it to Washington, D.C., to rally political support.

Although the official position of the Church of the Brethren was total objection to the armed conflict in Vietnam, they did not forbid members from joining the military. Many enlisted, and many Brethren served in Vietnam, much like the generation before—during World War II.

For a number of Brethren, though, war was simply not an option. Some attempted to wage peace on the front lines by serving with International Volunteer Service in Southeast Asia. They provided humanitarian aid, did refugee and relief work, and attempted to create awareness of the destruction and death caused by the military action. Each risked their life by serving in a war zone, and some lost their lives in the name of peace. Chandler Edwards, who trained with a Brethren Volunteer Service unit, was killed shortly after delivering supplies to a Laotian village in April 1969. Two years later, Ted Studebaker was gunned down by the Vietcong as he worked on an agricultural project with Vietnam's mountain people.

Closer to home, other Brethren volunteered their time and money for refugee work. They participated peacefully in protests, even when others lashed out violently against the government. The 1969 Annual Conference in Louisville, Ky., saw nearly 1,000 attendees march to the nearby federal building and hold a peace vigil in silence, probably the largest single Brethren display of peace witness to date.

These Brethren, drawing from the New Testament and their pacifist heritage, knew their duty was to choose peace. Seeking peace would not come without a cost. Some paid in jail time; some risked their professional careers to speak their minds. One young man lost the use of his legs. A few lost their lives. For many Brethren, speaking out against an unpopular war was not easy, but they chose to suffer rather than betray their convictions.

Sources: *The Brethren Encyclopedia, Messenger* (October 1979), *Annual Conference Minutes* (1964, 1966, 1967, 1972), and *Uniting Work and Spirit: A Centennial History of Elizabethtown College* by Chet Williamson.

2008 & beyond
What's next?

Cheryl Brumbaugh-Cayford

2008 & BEYOND

A variety of church leaders were invited to share brief reflections on their view for the path ahead: What are the trends? What should the priorities be? What might the next century hold?

"Vital and alive Brethren in the next century will be less concerned with the state of the denomination and more concerned with the state of the mission. Rather than focusing on the numbers in our pews, we'll celebrate the multitudes at work in the world. Instead of trying to narrow the limits of God's love, we'll generously share the radical love of Jesus with all we encounter. In the new century our focus will be less on what we have and need and more on our capacity to give and to share. Where in the past we built structures and created organizations, we will instead resource disciples and cultivate networks.

The primary ethic that will guide this outward-focused living is love. Because God first loved us, we have no choice but to join God in the work of love in the world. Love will motivate us to refute violence and foster reconciliation. Love will compel us to serve our neighbor, friend, and enemy. Love will inspire us to sing and to pray. Love will teach us to live lightly on the earth. Love will evoke creativity and artistry. Love will remind us to stoop and wash each others' feet. Love will empower us to lose our lives (personal and institutional) for the sake of the other, for the sake of God's world.

Another century of being "brethren" will be meaningful only if it means following the way of love, Jesus the Christ.**"**

–Jonathan Shively

"In the early years of the church, leaders were wary of higher education. Many believed that education and faith were incompatible because formal learning would lead students to accept sources of authority beyond the Bible. For those who believed that the Bible was the sole authority for all religious questions, the thought of academic study of the Bible was frightening.

As the Church of the Brethren began to establish its own colleges in the late 1880s, an important realization came to the denomination: Education opens minds. Education opens learners' minds to new epistemologies and new perspectives on common practices. It creates understandings about what it means to be the "outsider." By the 20th century, Dan West, Gladdys Muir, M.R. Zigler, Norman Baugher, Anna Mow, Andrew Cordier, Harold Row, A. Blair Helman, Dale Aukerman, Paul Robinson, Kermit Eby, Bob Neff, Don Durnbaugh, and scores of others demonstrated with their lives the powerful combination of faith and learning.

Faculty members at the Church of the Brethren colleges in the past and present know that with open minds often come open hearts. In the next century, continued investment in our colleges by the church and its families will lead to persons of ability and conviction who are problem solvers in a world that desperately needs their faith-based insights and motivations.

As we move into a century where global communication redefines what it means to be "neighbors," open minds and open hearts are increasingly essential. Education rooted in the values of simplicity, faith, and community empowers learners to understand that both the knowledge they gain and their faith commitment to work for "the glory of God and our neighbor's good" makes all the difference in the world.**"**

—Jo Young Switzer

"As we face the future as a denomination, we need to shift our mindsets from being a small church with limited influence to a people of God with potential to change the world. When we think small and negative, we fulfill our own self-declared destinies.

We should be a people of God who build around our strengths. What if David, the shepherd boy, would have said, "I can't." Instead, he confidently said to the giant, "You come to me with a sword and a spear and a javelin. But I come to you in the name of the Lord of Hosts." David thought the giant he faced was so big that with God's help he couldn't miss.

What percentage of Brethren people think about playing to their strengths? Or do we succumb to the negatives of what we wish we would do but can't? We will grow the most where we are already strong. We need to build on our strengths. What unique people is God calling us to be, and what ministries is God calling us to do? Can we, on the national level, the district level, and in our local congregations, be more visionary and permission-giving without too much concern about bureaucracy? Our biggest challenge is to be open to God's Spirit, who will lead us into uncharted waters and into the wilderness of potential. **"**

—Earl Ziegler

"The Church of the Brethren has a unique and historical combination of Pietism (personal, Spirit-filled faith-life) and Anabaptism (importance of the community of faith). This combination has been manifest in the way the church has maintained a mix of grassroots organizational structure and a strong cultural identity.

We inhabit a culture that is amazingly diverse and seeks communities of faith that can embrace that diversity. How does a once "peculiar people," who were known by the manner of their living and commonness of their clothing, maintain an identity in the midst of cultural diversity? An easy answer is to say we ought to embrace our core values, but even that is cause for debate. What does nonresistance look like today? What is simple living? Are we really together? What could possibly unify the Church of the Brethren for the next hundred years?

Jesus. In reality our core values are not "peace, simplicity, and togetherness." Those are ways we have tried to live out our real core value: taking Jesus seriously. To be sure, even as we have sought to follow in Jesus' way, from time to time that has led us in different directions. But I see a future for a group of believers who invites the world to join them in the journey of taking Jesus seriously, recognizing that there are a multitude of faithful responses to that effort. It is the effort of following where Jesus leads that brings us closest to being the body of Christ. And it just so happens that it offers an authenticity of faith for which this culture seems to desperately crave. The Church of the Brethren is made for this time and place. **"**

—Shawn Flory Replogle

"The image is winsome: Two little boys scaling three strands of barbed-wire fence to fly their kite. The boys and the artist, Estelle Ishigo, were Japanese Americans interned in a relocation camp by the US government during World War II. Ishigo's painting signifies the human spirit striving to break free whatever the odds.

The scene touches closer to home when we recall that Brethren were directly engaged with Japanese American internees, assisting them in their encampment and helping resettle them after the war. Just as in Armenia, where Brethren mounted aid for the survivors of genocide during and after World War I; in Spain, during the civil war of 1937-1938, where the nutrition needs of refugee children prompted the formation of Heifer International; in Germany, when refugees from World War II were destitute, and the sale of SERRV handcrafts was launched to provide income; in Brethren churches and homes in the 1960s that hosted Russian Orthodox Church delegations whose leaders were being vilified by politicians and religious critics here at home; and today, in North Korea, where Brethren support bolsters agricultural production in a hungry but enemy nation.

The community of founding Brethren was marked by a radical faithfulness that put it in tension with religious and governmental authorities. The drive for faithfulness prompted succeeding generations to forgo public favor as they reached out to the stranger, to the enemy, to groups fenced in or walled out. Their action was grounded in the Ephesians passage that says of Christ, "He is our peace" and that "he has broken down the dividing wall, that is, the hostility between us" (2:14).

My prayer is that coming generations of Brethren will be a reconciled and reconciling community that hungers and thirsts for justice. I pray that at the heart of that mission, that alternative cultural vision, will be the Christ who is called "our peace." And that two boys and a kite may serve to remind us of callings yet to come. **"**

–Howard Royer

"I love the Church of the Brethren.

At her knee I was taught that God wants me to live peaceably with all. I have watched her example over and over again as she has volunteered to feed the hungry, dig wells for the thirsty, visit those in prison, take care of the children in a crisis, and stand in solidarity with the underdog. She is the one who put her arm around my shoulder and said, "You are called to preach the good news of God's love."

I see this Church of the Brethren less and less. She seems to have been replaced by a group of factions all struggling to inherit the Church of the Brethren. But soon there will be nothing to inherit. It is time we get back to doing what Jesus did instead of struggling to survive and win. I want us to focus on saying no to hate; sitting down to eat with the marginalized; opening our churches to house the homeless; buying less and giving away more; and addressing the issue of why our prisons are overflowing—just to mention a few.

It is time to quit talking about Jesus and start following Jesus. **"**

–Susan Boyer

"I have been Brethren my entire life. When I was little, I always thought everyone on earth was Brethren. Now a youth, and very active in the church, I realize this is not true.

There are so many different sects of Christianity alone, and then the denominations! The list goes on and on. There are other religions. There are also non-religions, better known as "atheists." When I walk the halls of my high school, I am not exposed to very much diversity—nearly none at all. But when I take a leap outside my familiar hometown, I see people who need touched, people who need witnessing, and people who need Jesus.

The Church of the Brethren has always made service a main aspect of our ministry. But there is also the aspect of spreading the Word of God, which I believe is necessary in order to continue the work of Jesus. The Great Commission (Matt. 28:19-20) says, "Therefore, go and make disciples of all nations, baptizing them in the name of the Father and of the Son and of the Holy Spirit, and teaching them to obey everything I have commanded you. And surely I am with you always, to the very end of the age."

Every day, we believers are exposed to people who do not know the love of our Lord and Savior. They are drowning, and we aren't saving them. As we celebrate an incredible 300 years as a large church family, I believe we as a church need to reach out to others and invite them to celebrate the incredible Jesus Christ who is eternal. Not everyone on earth is Christian. **"**

–Seth Keller

"Beyond this tercentennial year, I look and pray for the continuance of covenant conversations that exhibit the strong biblical concept of forbearance. The New Testament Greek words translated as "forbearance" carry meanings akin to patience, self control, restraint, mercy, longsuffering, and refusal to threaten (Eph. 4:2; Col. 3:13; Eph. 6:9: 2 Cor. 12:6, etc.).

Historically we've used it and abused it. Old Annual Conference answers to queries sometimes urged the practice of forbearance. But forgetting about forbearance, we have sometimes championed specific interpretations of the Word as **"The Word,"** and have pressed for punitive discipline or disenfranchisement for those who disagree. In so doing, covenant conversation is too often reduced to name-calling, accusations of sinfulness, threatened lack of support, and even hints of covenant separation. Such times are not a proud part of our history.

Forbearance is not tolerance. Tolerance has the feel of superiority accepting inferiority. Forbearance is more open to possible understanding. Indeed, it represents a "standing with" response in the spirit of hope and openness toward common ground. Forbearance is a form of community acceptance that embraces the validity of different perspectives while being willing to continue dialogue in the hope of more widespread agreement.

Most of all, forbearance recognizes that service to Jesus Christ can be corporately uplifting and personally gratifying when experienced by those who do not agree 100 percent on the specifics of interpreting the One who blesses us and calls us into service in His name. We can faithfully roll up our sleeves and together practice love of God and love of neighbor without agreeing on jots and tittles.

–Earle W. Fike Jr.

"Paul's letter to the Galatians makes it quite clear that when you love God and follow Christ you will begin acting, thinking, and feeling in a new way. This new way will be evident by how you treat other people. Those who live their lives drenched in the love of God cannot help but allow that love to splash on others as well.

When we live in the power of the Spirit we don't love others because we have to; we love others because we can't help ourselves. It is who we are, it is what we do. It is as natural as breathing.

When we commit our lives to a God of love, grace, and generosity, then we too will become people of love, grace, and generosity. The Holy Spirit won't make us perfect. But it will make us more and more into the people God created us to be.

When people ask me if I think the Church of the Brethren will survive for another 300 years I am reminded of the words of the late Rev. William Sloan Coffin. When asked if he was optimistic about the future of the world he replied, "No, I am not optimistic. But I am hopeful." Coffin writes, "Hope has nothing to do with optimism. Its opposite is not pessimism but despair. And if Jesus never allowed his soul to be cornered into despair, clearly we Christians shouldn't either."

Coffin believed, "It's hope that helps us keep the faith, despite the evidence, knowing that only in so doing has the evidence any chance of changing."

So am I optimistic about the future of the Church of the Brethren? No I am not. But am I hopeful? Absolutely!**"

–Christy Waltersdorff

"It's been said that the river is purest at its source, and that seems to be true of the church. That is what the early Brethren wanted to recover. And accounts of their life together suggest that it did indeed resemble the life of the early church. That's why people were so attracted to them, while others hated them.

This passionate quest for spiritual renewal is the most beautiful part of the Brethren heritage. This is what we need to recover from our heritage. We do not necessarily need to recover all the forms and traditions of the past. We do not need to sing *a capella* all the time, or go back to plain dress. There is a sense in which we can never "go back," because God is always doing a new thing. With an infusion of new spiritual power, some of our traditions would be retained and infused with new life, while others might just fall away.

What we need is to recover that spiritual power that was characteristic of the early New Testament church, and of the early Brethren. During this anniversary celebration, we need to remember the spiritual power and practice of the early Brethren. We can also celebrate the good we see in the current Church of the Brethren. Keep in mind that the greatest resemblance to the spirit of the early Brethren may be found among the Dominican Brethren, Nigerian Brethren, other "third-world" Brethren, and our "ethnic Brethren" here in the US. They may be pointing the way back for us.

The early Brethren were passionate in their quest for spiritual renewal. Are we? **"**

–Bob Vroon

"Now that our 300th Brethren Birthday Party is over:

• *Have we caught something of the spiritual fervency of our Brethren forebears?* The Reformation, along with the Anabaptist and Pietist movements, were wonderful foundations for spiritual revival, which affected the early Brethren as they made deep commitments to live for Christ and to abide by the clear teachings of the New Testament. We need more of their spiritual fervency.

• *Do we blow out the 300 candles, cut the cake, walk away, and say, "It was a good party, but don't ask me to make any changes?"* Birthday parties are not events where much serious thinking usually takes place. It is an OK fun time, but not many revivals start at a birthday party.

• *Do we think our "world" is any safer than the one from which the early Brethren sought to separate?* Likely all of us have snickered a bit at some of their strange and unique ways. Will our accommodation to so much of present-day society leave anything for which future generations will remember us?

• *Are we clear in our understanding that salvation is not found in our Brethren heritage?* Salvation is found in Christ alone. Early Brethren leaders may be good examples for Christian discipleship, but they are not our saviors. They founded a Christ-centered church that happens to be called Brethren.

• *Will we use the Brethren "birthday party" occasion to invite more people into our spiritual family?* We usually start having birthday parties for children at age 1. It is proof that a new person has joined our family. May we go out with greater zeal to win many for Christ and the church. **"**

—James F. Myer

"As Jesus articulated the kingdom, it was marked by the character of God and God's passion for the world. Namely, in keeping with God's character and passion, the kingdom of God is a realm defined by love, compassion, and a deep concern for social justice. We are participants in God's kingdom when we live lives of love, compassion, and justice.

In the emerging paradigm, therefore, it is the manner of our living and commitment to the kingdom that relates us to God and transforms our lives. It is not buying into a particular set of beliefs or doctrines or creedal statements that brings us new life. It is following Jesus in proclaiming the kingdom. This was Jesus' challenge to the religious and political domination systems of first-century Palestine. And it got him killed.

So does the Church of the Brethren want to reverse its downward membership trend? Do we want to appeal to those millions of folks who want to be followers of Jesus, but for whom the earlier paradigm of traditional Christianity does not work? Then as a denomination we need to focus on and declare with vigor the kingdom of God as revealed by Jesus of Nazareth—a kingdom not of "beliefs," but a kingdom of love, compassion, and justice. **"**

—Galen Miller

"As noted by historian Don Durnbaugh, a critical part of what spurred the emergence of the early Brethren movement was attention to their immediate context—the currents roiling through church and society. Our historical context is not unlike that of our founders: war; environmental destruction; resource extraction at the expense of the poor or the indigenous; displacement of people due to conflict, ethnic tension, environmental demise, and simple greed.

Through our history, our awareness of the realities of our world has led to

remarkable contributions to service and peacemaking. In today's world, the stakes are so high, the chasms between us so large, the disintegration of creation so imminent, that more is needed.

If we pay attention to our historical context, we may well be compelled to look beyond traditional ministries of charity and service and even development as we commit ourselves to the work of justice and maintaining a global eco-culture that can sustain life. And finally we may find ourselves feeling compelled toward solidarity—standing with our global neighborhood as partners and co-creators of a more promising future.

The early 1700s was an opportune moment—it is such a moment now. People now as then are looking for something deeper, truer, enlivening, and people are acting. A number of recent books (*Blessed Unrest, The Great Turning, Deep Economy, The Bridge at the End of the World*) point to a groundswell of people who have seen that something isn't right with the way we're approaching life, and are rising to do something about it.

These stirring masses may just welcome a spiritual grounding for their awakening; they may just be waiting for someone to show them the way. **"**

—David Radcliff

CONTRIBUTORS

Alice Archer, of South Bend, Ind., is an ordained minister in the Church of the Brethren.

J. Douglas Archer, an ordained minister, is reference and peace studies librarian at the University of Notre Dame.

James Benedict is pastor of Union Bridge (Md.) Church of the Brethren.

Susan Boyer is senior pastor of La Verne (Calif.) Church of the Brethren.

Pamela K. Brubaker is professor of Religion at California Lutheran University, Thousand Oaks, Calif.

Christina Bucher is professor of Religious Studies at Elizabethtown (Pa.) College.

Logan Condon, a member of the Naperville (Ill.) Church of the Brethren, served as an intern in the Brethren Historical Library and Archives in Elgin, Ill.

Jane Davis, of Castle Rock, Colo., is an ordained minister in the Church of the Brethren.

Nevin Dulabaum is president of the Church of the Brethren Benefit Trust.

Earle W. Fike Jr. is a retired pastor, seminary teacher, and General Board executive, and a former Annual Conference moderator. He lives in Bridgewater, Va.

Tim Harvey is pastor of Central Church of the Brethren, Roanoke, Va.

Seth Keller, a member of Bermudian Church of the Brethren, East Berlin, Pa., was a member of the Church of the Brethren National Youth Cabinet.

Denise Kettering is assistant professor of Brethren Studies at Bethany Theological Seminary, Richmond, Ind.

J. Kenneth Kreider, professor emeritus of History at Elizabethtown (Pa.) College, is an author and a member of the Brethren Historical Committee.

Steve Longenecker is department chair and professor of History and Political Science at Bridgewater (Va.) College.

Galen Miller, of Wenatchee, Wash., is an ordained minister and retired Oregon/Washington District executive.

James F. Myer is an ordained minister in the Church of the Brethren and part of the free ministry team at White Oak Church of the Brethren, Manheim, Pa.

Janis Pyle, of Nevada, Iowa, is former coordinator of mission connections for the Church of the Brethren.

David Radcliff, of Elgin, Ill., is director of New Community Project.

Frank Ramirez is pastor of Everett (Pa.) Church of the Brethren.

Shawn Flory Replogle, pastor of McPherson (Kan.) Church of the Brethren, served as Annual Conference moderator in 2009-2010.

Paul Roth is pastor of Linville Creek Church of the Brethren, Broadway, Va.

Howard Royer is manager of the Church of the Brethren Global Food Crisis Fund.

Kenneth M. Shaffer Jr. is director of the Brethren Historical Library and Archives.

Jonathan Shively is executive director of Congregational Life Ministries for the Church of the Brethren.

Anna M. Speicher is project director and senior editor of the *Gather 'Round* curriculum project.

Jo Young Switzer is president of Manchester College, North Manchester, Ind.

Bob Vroon is pastor of Wilmington (Del.) Church of the Brethren.

Christy Waltersdorff is pastor of York Center Church of the Brethren, Lombard, Ill.

Gene Wampler is a member of Indian Creek Church of the Brethren, Harleysville, Pa. His brother, Joe Wampler, contributed to this article.

Walt Wiltschek is campus pastor/director of campus ministry for Manchester College, North Manchester, Ind. He was editor of *Messenger* magazine 2004-2010.

Earl Ziegler, of Lancaster, Pa., is a retired pastor and former Annual Conference moderator.